MONOGRAPHS OF THE
SOCIETY FOR RESEARCH IN
CHILD DEVELOPMENT

SERIAL NO. 220, VOL. 54, NOS. 3-4, 1989

THE MUTUAL EXCLUSIVITY BIAS
IN CHILDREN'S WORD LEARNING

WILLIAM E. MERRIMAN
LAURA L. BOWMAN

WITH COMMENTARY BY
BRIAN MAC WHINNEY

CONTENTS

ABSTRACT	v
I. THEORETICAL STATUS OF THE BIAS	1
II. EMPIRICAL STATUS OF THE BIAS	31
III. EXPERIMENT 1: DISAMBIGUATION BY YOUNG CHILDREN	58
IV. EXPERIMENT 2: DISAMBIGUATION, IMMEDIATE CORRECTION, AND RESTRICTION BY YOUNG CHILDREN	66
V. EXPERIMENT 3: IMMEDIATE CORRECTION AND RESTRICTION BY CHILDREN AND ADULTS—LINGUISTIC AND METALINGUISTIC MEASURES	82
VI. EXPERIMENT 4: YOUNG CHILDREN'S JUSTIFICATIONS FOR DISAMBIGUATION	102
VII. GENERAL DISCUSSION	105
REFERENCES	116
ACKNOWLEDGMENTS	123

COMMENTARY

MAKING WORDS MAKE SENSE, BY BRIAN MACWHINNEY	124
CONTRIBUTORS	130

ABSTRACT

MERRIMAN, WILLIAM E., and BOWMAN, LAURA L. The Mutual Exclusivity Bias in Children's Word Learning. With Commentary by Brian MacWhinney. *Monographs of the Society for Research in Child Development*, 1989, **54**(3–4, Serial No. 220).

Nearly every recent account of children's word learning has addressed the claim that children are biased to construct mutually exclusive extensions, that is, that they are disposed to keep the set of referents of one word from overlapping with those of others. Three basic positions have been taken— that children have the bias when they first start to learn words, that they never have it, and that they acquire it during early childhood. A review of diary and test evidence as well as the results of four experiments provide strong support for this last view and indicate that the bias develops in the months following the second birthday but does not gain full strength or become accessible to consciousness until sometime after the third birthday. Several studies also show that, after this point, it can still be counteracted by information in input or by a strong belief that something belongs to the extension of a particular word. The full body of evidence is compatible with the view that mutual exclusivity is the default option in children's and adults' procedures for integrating the extensions of new and old words. We present several arguments for the adaptive value of this kind of bias.

I. THEORETICAL STATUS OF THE BIAS

The focus of this *Monograph* is a claim that has guided much recent research on children's word learning—namely, that children are disposed to construct mutually exclusive extensions of the terms they acquire. An extension is the set of all referents of a word (Lyons, 1977), and two extensions are mutually exclusive if they have no members in common. Thus, our concern is with whether children are biased to keep words from sharing referents.

The following examples should make the concept of mutual exclusivity (henceforth referred to as ME) clearer. The extension of "cow" is mutually exclusive with those of some related nouns, such as "horse," "herd," "udder," and "farm," but not with those of others, such as "animal," "bovine," "Hereford," or "Bessie" (when used to refer to a cow). "Cow" is also mutually exclusive with all words that are not nouns (e.g., "brown"). Even though "cow" and "brown" could be said of the same thing, they are mutually exclusive because one refers to a whole object whereas the other refers to an attribute.

The remainder of this chapter concerns the status of the ME bias within different theories of children's word learning. In Chapter II, the empirical support for various hypotheses is examined; the rest of the *Monograph* is devoted to new data and conceptualizations.

Not all theorists have considered the ME bias explicitly, but most have made proposals that bear on its status. Even the explicit treatments have failed to consider certain logical implications of having the bias, and this failure may be at the root of certain controversies about it. Our review begins with a logical analysis of ways in which the bias could affect children's word learning, explicit treatments of the bias are then evaluated, and, finally, implicit treatments are considered.

POSSIBLE EFFECTS

The ME bias could influence children's word learning in four ways. First, a child's decision about the reference of a new word could be affected

(Markman & Wachtel, 1988). For example, suppose a child sees a gyroscope and a cup and is told, "Bring me the gyroscope." Even if the word "gyroscope" were unfamiliar, the ME-biased child would respond correctly: she would not select the cup, reasoning that it could not be called both "cup" and "gyroscope." Thus, if the referent of a new word is ambiguously specified, children should decide that it is something they cannot name rather than something they can. We call this the *disambiguation effect*. Responses that are compatible with this effect need not be correct—in the example just given, if the new word had been "demitasse," then the child's response would have been wrong.

Second, the bias might compel a child to change the extension of a familiar word (Barrett, 1978; Merriman, 1986b). If a new word were introduced for what the child believes to be a referent of a familiar word, he might correct this belief. For example, a child who thinks that a certain animal is a dog but hears it called "wolf" might react by removing wolves from the extension of "dog." We call this the *correction effect*. Such "corrections" need not always be right; for example, a child who heard "demitasse" for a particular cup could decide that it is wrong to call this object "cup."

Third, the bias might compel a child to reject a new word (Macnamara, 1982; Mervis, 1984). For example, a child who hears the new word "wolf" might respond, "No, dog." We call this the *rejection effect*. Although it is possible for such rejections to be appropriate (e.g., if someone actually misnamed something), they would be inappropriate in most cases.

Finally, the bias might influence word generalization: if something is known to have a particular name, children should not generalize other names to it (Merriman, 1986b). We call this the *restriction effect*. For example, suppose children see an object that is a cross between a cup and a glass (Labov, 1973). If told, "This is a glass," they would infer that it is not a cup; if told nothing, they would decide that it is either a cup or a glass, but not both. Responses that are compatible with this effect may or may not be correct.

Whenever a new word is introduced, the child needs to produce only one of the first three effects to preserve ME. For example, suppose she hears, "This is a frankfurter," and this name is unfamiliar. To produce the disambiguation effect, she needs to select an object that she has not already tagged, that is, one that is not the referent of a familiar name. This may not be easy to do, especially if cues such as speaker gaze and gesture indicate that a familiar object is the intended referent. However, even in such cases, there are other ways to disambiguate, for instance, by deciding that "frankfurter" refers not to a whole object but to some attribute such as color or texture. If she rejects these options, the child can maintain ME by producing the correction effect, that is, by taking the old tag off the object and deciding that what she thought was called a "hot dog" is actually a "frankfurter." The final option is rejection (i.e., refusing to put the new tag on)—she could insist, "That's not a frankfurter." Any one of these responses would preserve ME.

Unlike the others, the restriction effect must occur if ME is to be preserved: if children have an ME bias, they will not generalize more than one name to the same thing. Thus, there are only two "strict" ME predictions—the introduction of a new name for an old name's referent should result in either disambiguation, correction, or rejection; and a name should not be generalized to the referent of another name.

EXPLICIT TREATMENTS

Three basic positions have been taken concerning the ME bias—namely, that children have it when they first start to learn words (Barrett, 1978, 1986; Clark, 1987; Markman, 1987), that they never have it (Gathercole, 1987; Nelson, 1988), and that they acquire it during early childhood (Merriman, 1986b; Mervis, 1987). We hold this last view. In what follows, the theoretical proposals that have been advanced for each position will be critiqued in turn. In the final section, we develop an elaborate defense against the major criticism of our own view, that is, against the argument that development of the bias during the preschool years would be maladaptive. Central to this defense is our proposal that ME becomes the default relation in children's procedures for integrating the extensions of new and old names; this proposal guides our evaluation of the empirical evidence presented in subsequent chapters.

Biased from the Start

Barrett's initial contrast theory.—Although he referred to it as a "contrastive" hypothesis, Barrett (1978) was the first contemporary theorist to propose an ME bias in children's word learning. He argued that a fundamental flaw of the two dominant theories of the 1970s—semantic feature theory (Clark, 1973) and functional core theory (Nelson, 1974)—was the assumption that words are learned solely on the basis of positive examples. According to Barrett, negative examples—that is, things known not to be referents of a word—must also be processed; otherwise, extensions will remain too broad. Children must contrast negative examples with positive ones, that is, find the differences between them; once a dimension of difference is discovered, then the particular dimensional values of the positive examples become defining. For example, a child might notice that positive and negative examples of dog differ with respect to the sounds the animals make and, consequently, turn barking into a defining feature of "dog"; a new animal would then be called "dog" only if it could bark. Barrett proposed that even children who know only a few words use this contrast process to determine extensions.

The part of Barrett's theory most relevant to the ME issue concerns how children identify negative examples; namely, they consider any positive example of one word to be a negative example of all other words in the same semantic field. In Barrett's (1978, p. 209) own words, "Once a semantic field is established (e.g., 'animal'), the extensions of the words within that field (*dog, bear,* etc.) are identified by abstracting the contrasts between the referents of those individual words." Two words from the same semantic field "are mutually exclusive because they are contrastively inter-defined" (p. 208). Thus, Barrett's essential claim is that children impose ME between related words. He proposes a kind of de facto bias: ME is a consequence of children's tendency to contrast, but it is not necessarily the goal they have in mind when determining extensions. "Dog" and "bear" end up being mutually exclusive only because children make some difference between their referents a defining difference.

Barrett (1978, p. 209) also predicted something like the restriction effect: "A contrastive hypothesis predicts . . . that a word will not be overextended by a child to label an object for which that child has already acquired a more appropriate name." Children would make the mistake of calling a squirrel "kitty," for example, only if they had not yet learned "squirrel." However, this predicted effect is less general than the restriction effect. The latter prohibits overlap not only between an overextension and a correct extension but also between two overextensions (e.g., calling a plum both "ball" and "apple") or two correct extensions (e.g., calling a blanket both "blanket" and "cover"). As Gathercole (1987) has noted, it is not clear whether Barrett thought children would also avoid these kinds of overlaps.

Barrett's contrastive hypothesis is not strictly entailed by his argument that, if children did not contrast positive and negative examples, they would never correct their overextensions. Even if this were true, it does not follow that children must always contrast; they only need do so eventually. Suppose a child calls shorts "pants" and learns "shorts" but does not immediately contrast the two words. Although he may continue to overextend "pants" to shorts for a while, he will stop if he eventually contrasts the words. This argument applies to any overextension the child might make with "pants"— the given error will stop once he contrasts the appropriate name with "pants."

Although the always-versus-eventually distinction may seem minor, it does have implications for whether the child, or the environment, is considered primarily responsible for imposing ME as well as for whether an ME bias needs to be present from the beginning of word learning. If it were always necessary to contrast words, then the child would have to be largely responsible for doing so and would have to do so from the beginning since contrastive input such as "Those are shorts, not pants" is infrequent. However, because only eventual contrast is necessary, an ME bias may not be needed, at least not from the beginning. Children may eventually receive contrastive input about the words that they mistakenly allow to overlap. Moreover, such input may have generalized effects. The child who is told, "That's a horse, not a dog," might not only stop calling horses "dog" but also stop using "dog" for other large animals. Thus, to learn a word's extension, it may not be necessary to receive corrective input about all other words that might be allowed to overlap.

One could still argue that the notion of an ME bias is useful for explaining why children are such efficient word learners. Although they need to contrast words only eventually, they would acquire correct extensions faster if they had the bias. Socializing agents would not have constantly to monitor and correct errors or to explain what the contrasts between particular words are; children would do so themselves. This kind of efficiency argument, which is intended to justify a proposed innate (or at least early developing) disposition, has been quite common to theories of language acquisition ever since Chomsky's (1959) critique of Skinner's (1957) *Verbal Behavior*. As Chomsky pointed out, although an exceedingly large number of wrong hypotheses are consistent with the linguistic input they receive, children induce the correct hypotheses very rapidly. They must therefore be disposed to consider certain hypotheses before others (i.e., to constrain the hypothesis space; Markman, 1987; Nelson, 1988); moreover, their favored hypotheses turn out to be the ones with the greatest probability of being correct for any particular language.

Barrett's revised theory.—Barrett (1982, 1986) subsequently elaborated his theory by proposing that the contrast process occurs at the end of a sequence of processes. The child first learns that a word names a prototypical referent, usually the thing that adults most frequently call by that name (see Bowerman, 1978). He then analyzes the prototype, isolating some of its features. Next, he assigns the word to a semantic field on the basis of the similarity of these features to those abstracted for other words, and, finally, he contrasts the prototype with those of other words in the field.

Barrett proposed the "precontrastive" processes to accommodate evidence that children can learn a new word from a single positive example and revise its meaning on the basis of additional examples (Bowerman, 1978; Nelson & Bonvillian, 1978). According to Barrett (1982, p. 320), after a child analyzes a word's prototype, "the child may begin to extend the word to novel referents on the basis that these new referents possess features that are similar to the identified features of the prototypical referent."

Although these revisions solve some problems, they also create a new one by removing an assumption crucial to the prediction that overextensions will be corrected as soon as appropriate names are acquired—namely, that an old and a new name will be contrasted as soon as the new name is learned. According to the revised theory, several processes intervene between learning and contrasting a new word; no mechanism prevents violations of ME during this interval. Thus, a child who overextends "macaroni" to spaghetti and then learns "spaghetti" should continue mistakenly to believe that spaghetti is a referent of "macaroni" until she contrasts the two terms; this will not occur until she analyzes the prototype of "spaghetti" and assigns the term to a semantic field. Until then, ME will be violated.

Barrett (1982, p. 321) does not perceive the incompatibility between his revised account and his central prediction:

> If the child has already acquired a more appropriate name for an object, then this theory would suggest that the child has compared the prototypical referent of this name with the prototypical referents of the other words in the same semantic field, and has identified the features that distinguish these referents from one another. It therefore follows that these other words should not then be overextended to label the objects that fall within the extension of that name, because the extensions of these other words have been differentiated from the extension of that name.

We challenge the first sentence. In the same text, Barrett argues that children may begin to generalize a new name before contrasting it with others. If so, the central prediction will not be in force during the precontrastive period, and the new name may be generalized into the extensions of the old names, and vice versa.

The revised theory and the central prediction could be reconciled by proposing that children proceed through the precontrastive processes very rapidly and, hence, correct overextensions relatively soon after acquiring appropriate names. Another solution would be to argue that children have more than a de facto bias, that is, that ME is not simply a consequence of the contrast process but rather a condition that children are directly motivated to maintain. Others have made this argument, and their positions will be reviewed later. However, it should be noted here that, if children were so motivated, Barrett's central prediction would be preserved, but his proposed stage of processing in which a word is assigned to a semantic field would become unnecessary. The process of monitoring whether using a word for a new object would violate ME serves the function of this stage, which is to group together words for contrasting. The child would know to contrast a new word with some old word if he sensed a "threat" to ME, that is, if one of the old word's referents resembled the new word's prototype enough for the new word to apply. By dispensing with the linguistic construct of semantic field, this solution would sidestep the criticism that the construct has drawn (for these criticisms, see Gathercole, 1987; and Nelson, 1979).

The analysis presented thus far brings to light an unfortunate possibility—namely, that, even if a child had an ME bias, both of the "strict" ME predictions could be disconfirmed in that she might allow the references of two names to overlap for some period before trying to impose ME on them. This possibility is unfortunate because it complicates the enterprise of testing for the ME bias (see Chap. II). A particular ME hypothesis will be testable only if it specifies the conditions under which the bias is expressed as well as its strength relative to other interpretative dispositions that children might have. The bias cannot have absolute strength; if it did, people would never learn the correct relations between words that are supposed to share referents.

Because the claim that children have a limited bias is not falsifiable, one might be tempted to dismiss research on ME since a particular "disconfirming" finding can always be discounted by identifying a disposition that competes with the bias or by defining the circumstances that activate it more narrowly. However, the notion of a limited ME bias has theoretical utility: although it is not falsifiable, specific accounts of how a limited bias affects children's word processing are. Some such account, perhaps one containing substantive predictions (such as those of Markman, 1987, and Merriman, 1986b, which are discussed later), may prove valid. Moreover, although not absolute, the ME bias may be so strong that it is activated in a broad range of circumstances and often overrides other dispositions. Thus, it is important to test for the various ME effects across a wide range of persons, words, referents, and instructions to find out how strong the bias might actually be.

Markman's perspective.—Markman (1984, 1987; Markman & Wachtel, 1988) has also proposed that young children have an ME bias. Her position differs from Barrett's in two respects—her justification for the bias is novel, and she acknowledges limits on the bias. Because of these differences, her predictions are also different.

Markman's (1984, pp. 403–404) justification of the bias is framed in terms of category usefulness:

> In order for categories to be useful they will tend to exclude each other to a fair degree. If an object could be a member of just about any category, then the categories would tell us little about the objects. In contrast, to the extent categories are informative about objects, to the extent that they contain much correlated information, they tend to be mutually exclusive. For example, an object cannot be a cat *and* a dog or a bird or a horse, and so on.

One problem with this argument is that category usefulness does not depend entirely on category informativeness; in fact, many have argued that the most useful categories are not the most informative ones (Anglin, 1977; Brown, 1958; Rosch, Mervis, Gray, Johnson, & Boyes-Braem, 1976). Informativeness is essentially the same as specificity (cf. Medin, 1983); thus "car" is less informative than more specific terms, such as "Camaro," because it excludes fewer other categories (e.g., "Corvette" and "Accord" are excluded only by "Camaro"). "Camaro" conveys all that "car" does (e.g., has a steering wheel) as well as additional information (e.g., is sporty). However, "car" may be more useful than more specific names because we are more likely to want to speak about cars in general than about particular models (Anglin, 1977; Brown, 1958). According to Rosch, Mervis, et al. (1976), basic-level categories, such as car, are more useful than highly specific ones because usefulness depends not only on how similar category members are to one another but also on how dissimilar they are to members of other categories. Categories that are very specific tend to be too similar to other categories and thus too likely to be confused (e.g., Camaros are much more easily confused with Corvettes than cars are with trucks). In fact, children tend to learn basic-level categories earlier than more specific ones (cf. Mervis, 1984; Mervis & Rosch, 1981).

If children are motivated to maximize usefulness rather than specificity, they should violate ME on those occasions when they have to choose between maintaining a basic-level extension that violates ME and reconstructing a narrower extension that preserves it. For example, suppose a child who had a fairly accurate extension for "car" heard the new word "Camaro" and neither rejected this new word nor misinterpreted it as a name for something other than a whole object (e.g., a part). He should allow "car" and "Camaro" to overlap rather than revise the extension of "car" to exclude Camaros. Thus, there should be instances in which children's basic-level bias overrides their ME bias and they neither disambiguate, reject, nor correct but allow two names to share referents.

Markman's acknowledged limits on the ME bias include that it may be overridden when a new word is subordinate to a familiar word (e.g., as "Camaro" is to "car"). However, her rationale is not based on a basic-level bias; rather, she has argued that children make a *categorical relations assumption*—that the extension of a new noun will constitute a category of whole objects—that comes into conflict with their ME bias whenever a new word is heard for the referent of a familiar one. They resolve this conflict by violating either ME or categorical relations. For example, if they hear "vehicle" for what they call "car," they can violate ME by allowing the terms to share referents, or they can violate categorical relations by misinterpreting "vehicle" as a name for a collection, attribute, or part (Markman & Wachtel,

1988). The latter is an instance of the disambiguation effect. According to Markman (1984, pp. 404–405),

> Which assumption is relinquished probably depends on the relative difficulty of fulfilling each. When the similarity among the objects is great and easy to perceive, then children will likely preserve the assumption of categorical relations and violate the assumption of mutual exclusivity. . . . When the category similarity is difficult to discern, as in superordinate-level categories, then imposing a part-whole structure would simplify the hierarchy and preserve the assumption of mutual exclusivity.

Markman's (1984) argument that children will allow a new word to be subordinate to a familiar one because the similarity among the members of a subordinate category is easy to perceive has a problem; namely, it does not explain why they forgo the option of preserving both the ME and the categorical relations assumptions by transferring some of the extension of the familiar word to the new one (e.g., deciding that some of the things they thought were called "car" are actually called "Camaro"). In other words, Markman does not explain why children would not produce the correction effect.

The second limit acknowledged by Markman is that the ME bias can be overridden by contradictory input. She noted (1987, p. 284) that, "If a parent repeatedly specifies, for example, that a poodle is a kind of dog, that might help the child overcome his or her initial reluctance to map two category terms onto the same object." Contradictory input can also override the categorical relations bias. For example, children will be less likely to maintain categorical relations when a new word is embedded in a syntactic frame that is characteristic of attribute words (e.g., "This is X" rather than "This is an X") or when its referent has a very salient attribute (Markman & Wachtel, 1988). Thus, Markman's general position is that resolution of the conflict between ME and categorical relations depends on the evidence for each and on the difficulty of maintaining the given bias.

Although discussion of empirical data is postponed to the next chapter, one piece of evidence cited by Markman (1984, 1987) serves to illuminate an important relation between the ME bias and the kinds of words toddlers know and hear. Markman has noted that toddlers know mostly basic-level words that are supposed to be mutually exclusive (e.g., they know "dog," "cat," and "horse" but not "animal" or "cocker spaniel"); similarly, most of the words presented to them by parents are basic level (Anglin, 1977; Mervis, 1984). There is thus a good match between the ME bias and the words toddlers know and hear. If they consistently maintained ME, they would be

(1) less likely to overextend words, (2) more likely to correct overextensions, and (3) more likely to retain information about new words. Condition 1 is a consequence of both the disambiguation and the restriction effects for basic-level words. Suppose a parent specifies the referent of a new basic-level word, "cow," ambiguously. The child who applies the ME principle increases her chances of identifying the correct referent by eliminating all potential referents known to belong to the extensions of other words. Thus, if she sees a horse next to the cow and knows "horse," she should not mistake "cow" to be a name for the horse; and, if the referent of "cow" had been clearly specified, she would not mistakenly generalize the name to similar animals that she knows to be referents of other basic-level names. Condition 2 is a consequence of the correction effect. If a parent first uses "cow" to refer to what the child mistakenly believes is called "horse," the child will react by correcting this mistake. Finally, condition 3 is compatible with Markman's usefulness justification. An ME-biased child should be motivated to figure out how the referent of a new word is different from those of a related familiar word; consequently, she may attend more closely to it and retain more information about it. If she lacked the ME bias, she might assume that the new word meant approximately the same thing as some familiar one and not attend as closely.

When input and the child's vocabulary no longer contain primarily basic-level words—as is the case for children aged more than 3 years (Adams & Bullock, 1986)—an ME bias might actually hinder word learning. Thus, a 3-year-old who knows "horse" and hears the new word "palomino" used with ambiguous reference might incorrectly infer that "palomino" is a name not for the horse she sees but for something else. If the referent were not ambiguous, she would decide either that palominos do not belong in the extension of "horse" or that the input about "palomino" should be rejected.

Flavell, Green, and Flavell (1986) and Markman and Wachtel (1988) have provided a cognitive developmental account that complements the preceding analysis. They have argued that cognitive limitations prevent young children from considering word interpretations that are not mutually exclusive; because of an inability to coordinate mental representations, they cannot conceive of something either as belonging to two categories or as having two names. Flavell et al. have proposed that young children's tendencies to impose ME, to reduce several perspectives of an array to a single perspective, and to equate appearance and reality incorrectly may all be manifestations of the inability to coordinate representations. Developmental increase in this skill allows them to construct overlapping extensions at older ages.

Markman and Wachtel (1988, pp. 154–155) make it clear that, although the ME bias may diminish, it probably never disappears:

It seems unlikely, however, that the mutual exclusivity principle is abandoned at some age, never to be used again.... When hearing a novel label in the presence of an object with a known label and an object without a known label, adults too would likely interpret the term as referring to the as yet unlabeled object. Although the assumption probably persists into adulthood, it might weaken with age or experience, as the speaker learns that many categories are organized into class-inclusion hierarchies and overlapping sets. Another possibility is that from quite early on, children and adults have the capacity to override mutual exclusivity, on a case-by-case basis, as long as there is enough evidence that it should be violated.

Clark's contrast theory.—Like Barrett, Clark (1983a, 1983b, 1987, 1988) has proposed that young children contrast new words with familiar ones. However, Clark's proposal is fundamentally different from Barrett's (cf. Gathercole, 1987) in that she uses "contrast" to mean "make different," whereas Barrett uses it to mean "make incompatible." Thus, Clark's proposal is weaker than Barrett's since there are many ways in which children can make the meanings of two words different without also making them incompatible. For example, "cop" and "policeman" share many referents yet differ in connotation (e.g., "cop" is less polite). A child who interpreted the new word "policeman" as differing only in connotation from the familiar word "cop" would be violating Barrett's contrast principle but not Clark's. Thus, Clark's central hypothesis is that children assume that the meaning of a new word will differ in some way from those of familiar words.

Clark has only recently made clear the relation between her contrast hypothesis and the ME hypothesis (cf. Clark, 1987, 1988; Gathercole, 1987; Merriman, 1986a). Because she proposed that children initially make both hypotheses but eventually abandon ME, we have classified her theory as containing the explicit hypothesis that children begin language acquisition with an ME bias.

Clark (1987, p. 26) has noted that ME actually entails contrast:

While Mutual Exclusivity superficially appears to be equivalent to the Principle of Contrast, it actually embodies two other principles besides. And even when children leave off using that part of Mutual Exclusivity captured in the Single Level Assumption, they continue to rely on Contrast.

She maintains that the ME bias is the conjunction of three biases—namely, that no two words mean the same thing (Contrast), that semantic fields have only one level of contrast (Single Level), and that words at one level in a semantic field denote nonoverlapping categories (No Overlap). According to Clark (1987, p. 26),

What Markman argued, in effect, is that children have a Single Level Assumption, which they give up as they learn terms at different levels. Children do not give up either the Principle of Contrast or the Principle of No Overlap. So by recasting Markman's hypothesis in this form, we can see what assumption it is that children actually give up and what it is they retain.

We disagree with this analysis because the construct of semantic field is not necessary to an explication of the ME bias. As we have already argued, children may have no notion of semantic field yet take care to keep word extensions from overlapping.

Although Clark attributes the ME hypothesis to Markman, her own version is unique. First, whereas she argues (1987, 1988) that once children acquire hierarchically related terms they stop assuming that words will be mutually exclusive, Markman and Wachtel (1988) argue that the ME bias weakens with development but probably never disappears. Second, she offers unique explanations for why young children are ME biased. One is that "children don't appear to realize that contrast operates both within and between levels for the lexicon and the grammar" (Clark, 1987, p. 12). This cognitive explanation, which stresses lack of awareness of relational possibilities, differs from Markman's (1987), which stresses inability to coordinate representations.

Clark (1983a, p. 72) offers a second unique explanation in her discussion of how the new word "cow" could correct the overextended old word "dog":

> Notice that children could start out thinking that the word "dog" was simply a superordinate, and so set up a partial inclusion relation between "cow" and "dog" when they add the word "cow." But that would leave half the domain without any label at the same level as "cow" and therefore constitute a gap in the child's taxonomy, as in (i):

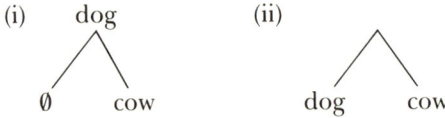

Instead, children seem to assume that "dog" and "cow" (and subsequent terms added to this domain) apply at the same level, as in (ii), and hence contrast with each other.

According to Clark, children may impose ME because they want to avoid creating lexical gaps, that is, categories that have no labels. (A corollary that

Clark, 1983a, 1987, has also endorsed is that children's tendency to invent new words is the result of their desire to fill lexical gaps.) There is a problem with Clark's analysis, however. The child who interprets "cow" as mutually exclusive with "dog" avoids one lexical gap but creates another—the superordinate category that includes the referents of both words. In Clark's example, there is no term at the top of the node in ii. Thus, to construct a valid justification for the ME claim from Clark's argument, one has to propose that children are more motivated to prevent same- than different-level lexical gaps. This proposal would be more credible if arguments could be made for why same-level gaps are less desirable than different-level ones. In fact, both have their disadvantages. If one allows a same-level gap, it is difficult to refer to the category of dogs-that-are-not-cows; however, if a different-level gap is created, it is difficult to refer to the category of dogs-and-cows.

According to the basic-level theory analysis presented in the previous section, and contrary to Clark's prediction, children should sometimes find a same-level lexical gap to be preferable to a different-level one. For example, if they considered cows to have only one or two properties that distinguish them from other four-legged animals, then neither cows nor other four-legged animals would constitute basic-level categories (which, by definition, must be highly discriminable from each other). Thus, children should be reluctant to change their basic-level categorization of "dog" into a non-basic-level one just because a new name has been introduced for a category member and should either reject "cow" or interpret it as overlapping with "dog."

As one reviewer of this *Monograph* noted, if Clark's contrast hypothesis were disconfirmed, then so would the ME hypothesis because the one entails the other. Clark's hypothesis has been thoroughly criticized by Gathercole (1987), and, if these criticisms were taken to disconfirm it (an issue addressed in later sections), there would be no reason to bother with the ME claim. However, it should be noted that Clark and Gathercole do agree in viewing Clark's hypothesis as irrefutable, albeit disagreeing about whether this is a good thing. According to Clark (1988, p. 322):

> To show sameness of meaning all down the line, one has to eliminate any possibility of difference. This in turn requires constant checking, to make sure the terms in question have the same extensions and the same distribution across contexts. Since differences in meaning may be subtle, it may take speakers a long time to discover that "little" and "small," "marsh" and "slough," or "often" and "frequently" do differ in meaning. To reject Contrast, that is, to accept the Null Hypothesis, imposes an immense burden on speakers, to establish the *absence* of differences in meaning.

MONOGRAPHS

Gathercole (1987, p. 499) concurs:

> Even if children were shown to use two or more words for exactly the same referents in exactly the same contexts, it would be near-impossible to disprove that those words do not *mean* the same thing for those children, and even more difficult to disprove that children *assumed* that those words meant different things.

Because Clark's contrast hypothesis cannot be disconfirmed, its fate cannot affect the status of the ME hypothesis directly.

Never Biased

Gathercole's critique.—Having evaluated the evidence and arguments for Barrett's and Clark's contrast theories, Gathercole (1987) concluded that (1) the available data on children's language do not support these theories, (2) two among their proposals have conceptual problems, and (3) children's correction of overextension can be explained without reference to a contrast bias. According to Gathercole, these conclusions hold whether one uses Barrett's sense of "contrast," which implies ME, or Clark's, which does not; however, her critique is more damaging to specific aspects of these two authors' theories than it is to a general ME hypothesis.

Her first conclusion is based on the well-replicated findings that children occasionally allow extensions to overlap (see Chap. III). These, however, do not strictly entail her conclusion. Children can both have an ME bias and allow such overlap (Markman & Wachtel, 1988); if given information that contradicts ME, they may resist their bias. For example, if told, "A dog is an animal," they are likely to decide that these names share referents. The only prediction entailed by a general ME hypothesis is that ME will be imposed when no other beliefs or biases conflict with it. An additional important point to note is that some of the studies reviewed by Gathercole failed to yield only one of the specific effects of the ME bias, such as the correction effect. As we noted earlier, the association between the bias and some of its effects is rather loose—when a new word is introduced for an old name's referent, a child need only either to disambiguate, or to correct, or to reject.

Gathercole identified several problems in two proposals made by Barrett and Clark. The first proposal, which is primarily Barrett's, is that young children establish semantic fields; the second, which is only Clark's, is that children coin new words to fill lexical gaps. Gathercole criticized the first proposal for lack of clarity, for incompatibility with evidence that only older children construct semantic fields, and for being unnecessary to explain why children correct overextensions once they learn new words. These criticisms are sound. However, Barrett's semantic field hypothesis is not a necessary condition for all versions of the ME hypothesis; in fact, our proposals for improving the compatibility between Barrett's revised theory and his central prediction entailed doing away with the semantic field hypothesis. Likewise, although Gathercole's criticisms of Clark's lexical gap hypothesis are persuasive, this hypothesis is logically independent of the ME hypothesis.

In reaching her third conclusion, Gathercole argued that children's correction of overextension can be attributed either to input or, in the case of basic-level object words, to preexisting concepts. As for the former, she noted that children occasionally receive explicitly corrective input; also, she took studies by Carey and Bartlett (1978) and Merriman (1986b) to show that children will correct their extensions in response to subtle kinds of input. Such an interpretation of these studies, however, is problematic. Only two subjects responded to Carey and Bartlett's input by imposing ME. In Merriman's study, the youngest children (2½-year-olds) were responsive only to explicit correction; the older ones (4- and 6-year-olds) were responsive to subtle input, but only if it indicated that the ME assumption was wrong—those in the no-additional-input condition showed a correction effect that was just as strong as among those who received input emphasizing word differences.

Gathercole's second explanatory construct, preexisting concepts, is equally problematic. According to Gathercole (1987, p. 524),

> Words for natural-object categories may appear to be used "contrastively" by the child since the concepts encoded by those words will be easily differentiated. Explaining any "contrastive look" to natural basic-level object words in this way would also account for the difficulty of finding a "contrastive look" in children's acquisition of fabricated words for made-up categories in experimental settings.

According to this argument, the results of Merriman's (1986b) artificial word learning experiment should not have supported the ME hypothesis—in fact, however, a substantial correction effect was found in older children. Gathercole's explanation of overextension correction in terms of preexisting concepts is also difficult to reconcile with Mervis's (1984) evidence that preexisting child-basic concepts do not always match the adult word meanings that children are supposed to learn.

Nelson's critique.—Nelson (1988) challenged the general notion that young children adhere to constraints when they generate word meanings, arguing that the empirical data on children's word learning are not compatible with either an ME, a contrast, or a categorical relations constraint. Like Gathercole (1987), she suggested that children's word learning can be satisfactorily explained in terms of input (or, more generally, "social guidance") and preexisting concepts.

A major limitation of Nelson's critique is that she focuses on the evidence regarding constraints and does not concern herself with biases. According to Nelson (1988, p. 228), "constraint" is the stronger term:

> A true constraint would be manifested in all or none type responses; bias is manifested in statistically significant trends that fall short of universally consistent response patterns. . . . If it is found that alleged constraints do not constrain but merely bias the learner, the term is misleading and suggests an innatist view of human development that may be unintended.

Nelson's arguments against an ME constraint do not hold up well against an ME bias. Her points are based on Gathercole's (1987) review, which we have already addressed, and on data presented in the next few chapters (which were summarized in conference papers by Merriman, 1987, and Merriman & Bowman, 1987); we will argue that, in fact, these data support the view that an ME bias develops during early childhood. Nelson (1988, p. 34) did acknowledge that children might acquire certain biases during the preschool years but noted that "it is only the weaker principle of contrast that should emerge at all, since the stronger principle of mutual exclusivity would lead the child acquiring a complex lexical system seriously astray, given the existence of overlap in terms at different hierarchical levels." This criticism will be addressed in the next section.

Biased after a While

Merriman's proposals.—Because he found that 4- and 6-year-olds tended to show the correction effect in a noun-training experiment but that 2½-year-olds did not, Merriman (1986b) proposed that the ME bias is not present from the beginning of word learning but does emerge during the preschool years. He presented two arguments for this proposal; one is cognitive in nature, and the other concerns the effects of linguistic experience. The cognitive argument (Merriman, 1986b, p. 950) runs as follows:

> The development of the tendency to contrast a new name with an old name may depend on improvements in conceptual processing. A central theme of theories of cognitive development (Fischer, 1980; Piaget, 1970; Sugarman, 1982) is that the child becomes increasingly capable of coordinating concepts. A child coordinates concepts if the child believes that the nature of one concept affects the nature of another. In the present experiment, only the older children may have coordinated the

concepts associated with the two names. Only the older children considered the possibility that information about the new name might necessitate a reinterpretation of the old name.

(Note that Merriman uses "contrast" in this passage in the same sense as Barrett, 1978, i.e., to mean "make incompatible with.")

Although its conclusion is incompatible with the one reached by Flavell et al. (1986) and Markman and Wachtel (1988), Merriman's argument appeals to the same construct—namely, the ability to coordinate mental representations. There may be an element of truth in both positions. Young children may be unable to understand how something can belong to two categories (which is Markman and Flavell's assertion) and also may tend not to think about a thing's membership in one category when considering whether it belongs to another (which is Merriman's proposal), failing to realize that the introduction of a new name for an old name's referent is the presentation of a second representation for it. Thus, children may have two deficits in conceptual coordination that have opposite implications for how they relate word extensions to each other.

An implication of this attempt to reconcile cognitive arguments that lead to opposing conclusions is that young children's maintenance of ME will depend greatly on the method of questioning: ME should be maintained when questions make it clear to children that they are to consider whether something belongs to more than one category. The questions used by Flavell et al. (1986) convey this request more clearly than those used by Merriman (1986b). Flavell et al. focused their subjects' attention on a single object, then asked, "What does this look like?" and, "What is it really?" Those who gave different answers to these two questions would almost certainly have realized that they had multiple representations of the object. In contrast, Merriman asked his subjects to pick out all the examples of one name from a set, returned the objects to the set, and then had them pick out all the examples of a different name. The subjects who picked overlapping sets of objects may not have realized that they had done so; when picking examples of the second name, they may have concentrated on how well the objects fit their representation of its meaning but failed to think about, or remember, how they had classified these objects vis-à-vis the first name.

This argument has empirical and theoretical grounding that extends beyond Merriman's own work. Sugarman (1987) presented children with a large set that contained four classes of objects and showed them that two objects, each from a different class, had stickers under them. When asked to find all other objects with stickers, only those older than 36 months attempted to eliminate classes of negative examples systematically. The younger children showed no realization that, if something was identical to a known negative example (something known not to have a sticker), then it also was a negative example. This result suggests that toddlers do not tend to think about an object's membership in one category when considering its membership in another. Karmiloff-Smith's (1986) research, discussed in a later section, also suggests that young children's thinking about one linguistic form is initially independent of their thinking about another. Finally, Merriman's argument is compatible with both processing-capacity accounts of cognitive development (Case, 1985; Fischer, 1980) and evidence that perceptual skill increases during preschool (DeMarie-Dreblow & Miller, 1988; Kemler, 1983). Because processing capacity increases with age, it may be that only older children have enough of it both to use a new name and to monitor its relation to other names. Also, if children will not maintain ME between two names when they cannot perceive properties that differentiate their referents, then in some cases only older children—who are the only ones able to perceive such properties—should maintain ME. Thus, even if children could not understand how something could belong to two categories, they might still assign an object to both.

A second way to reconcile the opposing conclusions of the cognitive arguments is to propose that some toddlers sidestep the multiple representation problem by giving a new name exactly the same meaning they had assigned to an old name—a solution that violates not only ME but also Clark's (1987) contrast hypothesis. By giving the same interpretation to two names, children do not have to coordinate representations. The results of Flavell et al.'s (1986) research can actually be viewed as supporting this proposal: young children often gave the same answers to the questions, "What does this look like?" and "What is it really?" which suggests that they interpreted "look like" and "is" to have overlapping reference, if not identical meaning. Also consistent with this interpretation is Merriman's (1986b) finding that 2½-year-olds were more likely to treat two trained names as synonyms than as any other type of pair (e.g., incompatibles, hyponyms).

Merriman (1986b) noted that the late emergence of the ME bias may have nothing to do with cognitive development; linguistic experience may be chiefly responsible. After numerous experiences in which an old name is corrected as a related new name is introduced, children may induce the rule that extensions should not overlap. There are many anecdotal reports of parents correcting old names and introducing new ones in the same breath, for example, "That's a turkey, not a chicken" (Barrett, 1986; Gruendel, 1977; Lewis, 1951). These kinds of parental responses seem to provide excellent support for the child's rule induction.

Mervis's arguments.—Mervis (1987, p. 226) also proposed that an ME bias does not emerge until some time after word learning begins, offering both a cognitive and an attitudinal argument. The former differs somewhat from Merriman's:

The metacognition required to realize that an object already assigned to one category should be assigned to another category . . . simply because a different label is used is quite complex. Note, too, that very young children do not understand much of the language that they hear. Therefore, when verbal input does not accord with the child's categories, it should be easy for the child to decide that he or she did not understand what was said, rather than deciding that his or her categorization scheme is incorrect.

Metacognitive development is necessary but not sufficient for development of the ME bias; an attitude change must also occur. Children have to accept the *expert principle*—namely, that adults "have authority on categorization issues" (Mervis, 1987, p. 227). Until they come to acknowledge adults' expertise, they will resist most of their elders' corrections. According to Mervis (p. 228), "After children acquire the expert principle, the exclusivity principle for basic-level categories should eventually follow."

There are some problems with this account. First, Mervis reduces the ME bias to the correction effect, and, as we have already noted, an ME-biased child need not show this particular effect (he might disambiguate or reject instead). Second, Mervis's proposal that young children will ignore a new name for an old name's referent is essentially a claim that they will show the rejection effect, yet she does not explain why children who lack an ME bias should show this effect. It cannot be argued that they would do so in order to prevent there being a new name with exactly the same meaning as an old one because—if they really believe that no two names can have the same meaning (Clark, 1987)—they would never consider the possibility of such an event happening. It is very difficult to argue that young children should show the rejection effect without also granting that they have some kind of ME bias (but see Chap. VII).

Adaptiveness.—One problem for the position that the ME bias develops during early childhood is that the effects of the bias seem to be maladaptive for preschoolers. In our discussion of Markman's proposals, we noted that it appeared that, although the bias might help children who were just beginning to learn words, it would probably hinder those who had already acquired a stock of mutually exclusive words. We will present arguments to show that neither of these propositions is necessarily true.

Why Toddlers May Not Need the Bias

We noted that, if toddlers had an ME bias, they would be (1) less likely to overextend words, (2) more likely to stop doing so, and (3) more likely to retain information about new words. There are several counterarguments with respect to the first function. First, if the bias were the only factor that limited name generalization, then toddlers who know only a few words would overextend excessively—in the absence of other constraints, a child with three words would map the entire world to one of these three (we are indebted to Michael Maratsos for this point). Thus, other biases must be operating, and toddlers may not need the additional help of an ME bias to avoid excessive error.

Second, one bias that toddlers do have is to avoid generalizing words to things that are perceptually dissimilar from known referents (Clark, 1983b; Markman & Hutchinson, 1984; Mervis, 1984). Because they have heard particular words applied fewer times and to fewer things than older children have, they should tend to generalize words less broadly (Merriman, 1986b; Nelson & Nelson, 1978) and hence be less prone to overextension than older children are.

Third, a child who has heard a word used for only one or two typical referents will overextend it less than one who has heard it used for many, especially if some of these are atypical (Mervis & Pani, 1980; Nelson & Bonvillian, 1973). If mothers avoid atypical referents in teaching names to their toddlers—as is indicated by Mervis's (1984) and White's (1982) observations—then toddlers should tend to overextend these names less often than older children do. Reich (1976) has even proposed that a long period of underextension in comprehension precedes the occurrence of toddlers' first overextension in production, and Rescorla (1980) found that a considerable period of correct production tends to precede a toddler's first overextension of a word. Thus, overextension tendencies may be minimal in the earliest phases of word learning.

Fourth, toddlers may be particularly conservative in name production, which would serve to limit their overextension tendencies further. Several studies of children's production of trained names have shown that, when input is controlled, toddlers generalize a name less broadly than older children do (for a review, see Nelson & Nelson, 1978). Although analogous studies of comprehension have yielded the opposite result (Merriman, 1986b; Merriman & Koshmider, 1987), toddlers may not be hindered by this tendency because they also tend to pick correct referents before overextended ones in comprehension (Kuczaj, 1982; Thomson & Chapman, 1977). The latter may protect them against errors in comprehending language addressed to them in natural discourse; for example, even if a toddler believed that both a cup and a glass could be called "cup," he would pick a cup rather than a glass when asked to pick "a cup."

Fifth, toddlers may use information in input to limit name generalization. Gelman and Taylor (1984) and Katz, Baker, and Macnamara (1974) have shown that 2-year-olds restrict their generalization of a new name for a doll if the name is not preceded by an indefinite article (e.g., "This is zav," rather than, "This is a zav"), apparently interpreting it as a proper name. Also, toddlers may be able to assimilate explicit name correction (e.g., "That's not a turkey"), and, as Brown and Hanlon (1970) observed, although parents tend not to correct their toddlers' syntactic errors, they do tend to correct overextensions and other semantic errors.

Finally, there is less need for the disambiguation effect (which limits misinterpretation of word reference) at this age. First, mothers tend to structure input so as to help toddlers identify referents by, for instance, pointing to or shaking an object in order to draw attention to it before naming (Messer, 1978) or naming distal objects only if both they and their toddler are looking at them (Collis, 1977). Second, Ninio (1980) observed that mothers nearly always name the objects in a picture before anything else and that their toddlers expect them to do this. Finally, because toddlers are attracted to novelty (Faulkender, Wright, & Waldron, 1974), they may find an object they cannot label to be more interesting than one they can. If so, they would not need the ME bias to produce the disambiguation effect: they would tend to interpret a new name as referring to an object they cannot label because they would tend to be looking at it when the name was introduced.

Toddlers might also be able to accomplish the second function we listed at the start of this section—that of correcting overextension errors—without an ME bias. First, parents have some tendency to correct overextensions (Gruendel, 1977; Leopold, 1939; Lewis, 1951; Rescorla, 1976). The rate of word learning is relatively slow at first but increases in a positively accelerating fashion (Templin, 1957), so they can successfully monitor the new words in their child's speech until the second birthday but not thereafter (Leopold, 1939; Rescorla, 1976). Because toddlers overextend only a minority of their words in production (Gruendel, 1977; Rescorla, 1976), and because such errors are salient (Anglin, 1977), parents may be able to identify and correct nearly all toddler overextensions. One weakness of this argument is the assumption that parents try to monitor their children's speech very closely when many, and perhaps most, do not. The next two arguments do not have this problem, however.

Young children might start using correct new names instead of incorrect old ones even if they did not immediately correct the latter. According to basic-level theory (Rosch, Mervis, et al., 1976), family resemblance—determined by the extent to which within- exceeds between-category similarity—is predictive of which of several correct names a speaker will prefer to use. Children's extensions for overextended names probably have only moderate family resemblance because they are heterogeneous sets; that is, they have low within-category similarity. In contrast, extensions of new names are likely to have greater family resemblance because most of these names are likely to have been heard for only one thing or a few similar things (yielding high within-category similarity). Thus, children may prefer new names over overextended old ones even if they allow the latter to remain overextended. For example, a child who extends "doggie" to all four-legged animals (a heterogeneous set) and then learns "cow" should prefer to call a cow "cow" rather than "doggie," not because he thinks "doggie" is wrong, but because the cow category has greater family resemblance than the four-legged animal category.

Finally, patterns of name input could also promote the development of a preference for correct new names. A child is more likely to observe others using a correct rather than an incorrect name. Each experience of hearing a correct name used for something should increase the probability of retrieving that name, rather than an overextended one, in subsequent encounters—if children hear only one word used for something, they should eventually follow suit. This proposal is compatible with MacWhinney's (1987) competition theory, discussed in a later section, and very similar to Leopold's (1939) explanation for the decline in his daughter's use of certain German words—namely, that, as she grew older, input became predominantly English.

The final putative function of the ME bias in toddlerhood that we listed at the outset is that it supports the motivation to learn new words. This is the weakest function of the three. First, when a new word is introduced for an old word's referent, the ME-biased child could decide to reject the new word instead of correcting the old one. Rather than attending closely to the differences between referents, the child might completely ignore the new word and its referent; indeed, toddlers have been observed to reject new names and to resist corrections of old ones (Merriman, 1986b; Mervis & Canada, 1983). If they strongly preferred rejection over correction, their word learning would actually be impeded. Second, they could decide to disambiguate rather than correct, and this also would be counterproductive; for example, if a child heard "cow" for what she calls "doggie," she could decide that "cow" is a name for a tail or a herd. Third, if toddlers lacked the ME bias but had the contrast bias that Clark (1987) has described, their motivation to learn a new word might not be undermined by information that it shares referents with another word. Even if told that a collie is a kind of dog, for example, they might still want to learn "collie" so they could say things about collies that they did not want to say about dogs in general. Finally, Bowerman (1985) has marshaled considerable evidence that children master new linguistic forms even when they have no obvious need for them; for example, they will learn a complex form of tag question even though they already know a simpler form that serves the same purpose.

How Older Children Could Be Helped by the Bias

Older children could be helped rather than hindered by an ME bias if it functioned as the default option in their procedures for integrating names, that is, if they assumed that a new name's extension was going to be mutually exclusive with others but could be convinced otherwise. If a conflict arose between this assumption and other beliefs, the tendency to maintain ME would be inversely related to the strength of the opposing beliefs, which would depend in part on the evidence presented to the child. Markman and Wachtel (1988) actually have a similar view of the bias in older children and disagree only regarding its status in younger ones.

A variety of conflicts between the ME bias and other beliefs can arise. If a child is told, "X is a kind of Y," where X is new and Y is old, three beliefs come into conflict—the ME bias, belief in speaker credibility, and belief in his own interpretation of input. He can resolve this conflict by abandoning one of the beliefs—by violating ME, by rejecting the speaker's authority, or by reinterpreting input (e.g., deciding that the speaker must have said, "X is kind of a Y"). If he challenges the speaker's authority, the rejection effect occurs. If he decides to reinterpret input, a variant of the disambiguation effect results. If he has reason to doubt either of the beliefs that conflict with his ME bias (e.g., he has observed the speaker make many naming errors, or he found the input difficult to hear), he should maintain ME.

When a child hears a new word for an old word's referent without being told about the relation between the two (e.g., is not told, "X is a kind of Y"), her ME bias conflicts not only with beliefs in speaker credibility and her own interpretation of input but also with her own representation of the old word's extension. If the latter is weak—for example, if she is uncertain about the appropriateness of the old name for the referent—she may decide to preserve ME by correcting the old name. Thus, children should overcome the ME bias only if other strong beliefs block the rejection, disambiguation, and correction options.

Input may not have to contradict ME explicitly in order to override the bias. Suppose a child who knows "horse" first encounters "palomino" in the sentence, "A palomino has a mane, makes neighing sounds, and loves to gallop." If she judged the speaker to be credible and the input to be clear, she would have difficulty imposing ME between "palomino" and "horse" because she knows of no difference between their referents.

Because of the limits on the ME bias, it is less of an obstacle to learning pairs of words with overlapping extensions than might be supposed. The bias will interfere with learning the second word of such pairs only if it is introduced by a speaker of low credibility, the reference of the introduction is ambiguous, or the child is uncertain of the old name's appropriateness.

The first two conditions should hold only rarely. Teachers and parents, who have high credibility for older children (Mervis, 1987), tend to make the relation of new words to old very clear, especially when the new word is superordinate (Adams & Bullock, 1986; Blewitt, 1983; Callanan, 1985; Shipley, Kuhn, & Madden, 1983). They tend to say things like, "A vehicle is something you drive around. A car is a vehicle, and so is a truck." Children would most likely abandon the ME assumption in response to this kind of input. The third condition is more likely to be realized, but it should not be in cases in which the referent of a new name is a *prototype* of an old one. Children should be fairly certain that old names apply to prototypes because these are the best examples of the names' categories. For example, a child should be so certain that a small rubber bouncing sphere is called "ball" that she should maintain this belief even if she hears it given the new label "sphere." The correction effect should be restricted to *atypicals* since children's beliefs about these are not as strong. For example, most who believe that a globe can be called "ball" should be somewhat uncertain because they realize that a globe is somewhat dissimilar to other balls. The introduction of the new word "globe" may be enough to convince them that their belief is wrong.

Correction effects for atypical referents should not always hinder word learning but might actually help in cases in which overextensions are corrected (e.g., children stop thinking that globes are a kind of ball because they learn "globe"). The effect on word learning would be negative only in cases in which underextensions are created (e.g., children stop thinking that chihuahuas are a kind of dog because they learn "chihuahua"). Thus, the overall value of the bias for older children depends in part on whether the set of all referents about which they are uncertain contains more incorrect than correct referents. If they were mostly uncertain about incorrect referents, then the bias would be quite useful.

Finally, it should be noted that a disposition to correct overextensions will be advantageous even if it entails a propensity to underextend. The problem of correcting linguistic overgeneralizations is much thornier than that of correcting undergeneralizations (Bowerman, 1987; Fodor & Crain, 1987; MacWhinney, 1987) because negative examples are identified for the child less frequently than positive ones are. A child who thinks that chihuahuas are not dogs will eventually stop believing this because he will eventually hear someone call a chihuahua-like dog "dog." However, a child who thinks that globes are balls may never be told that they are not. He may be told that a globe "is a globe"—an instance of positive exemplar input—but he will not infer from this that it is not a ball unless he has an ME bias. Moreover, because older children will have seen a greater variety of positive examples for any particular word, they will be more prone than younger ones to over- rather than to underextend. Thus, they stand to benefit more from having a bias that restrains overextension but encourages underextension. In fact, there is some evidence that, during early childhood, overextensions decline sharply but underextensions increase (Kendler & Guenther, 1980; Merriman, 1986b)—exactly the pattern one would expect if a general restriction on generalization were acquired during this period.

IMPLICIT TREATMENTS

Both Karmiloff-Smith (1986) and MacWhinney (1987) have developed general theories of how the representation and processing of language change during childhood. Although neither has addressed the issue of ME directly, the central proposals of each theory are compatible with some but not all expressions of the bias; for example, neither theory is compatible with the prediction that children will respond to a new name for an old name's referent by immediately correcting the old name.

MacWhinney's competition model.—The competition model is an elaborate information-processing account of language acquisition; although MacWhinney (1987) has primarily applied it to the acquisition of grammar, he has sketched some of its implications for word learning. He proposed that, every time a child either hears or uses a word for a particular referent, the association between the word and the referent becomes stronger; consequently, the word becomes a stronger "competitor" against other words as a name for that kind of referent. The frequency and consistency of word-referent pairing in input determine the speed and reliability of a child's retrieval of a word for a referent. One implication of this process is that repeated occurrence of a new word in input can cause the correction of an overextension (MacWhinney, 1987, p. 291):

> If the child finds that "raccoon" competes successfully for referents that he would have called "cat," he learns to restrict the range of "cat" by strengthening connections to "raccoon."

One problem with this account is that, although it explains why children will become less likely to produce a particular overextension, it does not explain why they eventually decide that it is wrong. Bowerman (1987, p. 452) made a similar point concerning the model's account of the correction of grammatical overgeneralizations:

> Where do intuitions of ungrammaticality come from? According to the competition account, the decline of *breaked, foots,* and the like is a matter of gradually decreasing activation strength. Presumably, activation strength never hits zero, since even adults occasionally produce forms

like these and they certainly hear them from children. Where in the downhill slide of *breaked* and *foots* do these forms pass over the boundary from being possible but simply less robust instantiations of notions of "*break* + PAST" and "*foot* + PLURAL" to being actively rejected as ungrammatical and unacceptable?

A further complication is that word pairs do not always become mutually exclusive. According to MacWhinney (1987, p. 295),

> When the child first hears the word "animal" used to refer to a dog, he initially senses a conflict between the words. . . . this conflict leads to a period of free variation. During this period, the child is receptive to any data that can distinguish the two forms.

Because the child hears "animal" used for a diverse set, he eventually constructs a broad extension for it that includes that of "dog." Thus, words become mutually exclusive only if they are presented in input for mutually exclusive sets. Only a very mild form of the ME hypothesis is therefore implied by the competition account—namely, that children sense conflict when two words seem to share referents and consequently become sensitized to information that might differentiate them.

Karmiloff-Smith's representational explicitation theory.—According to Karmiloff-Smith (1979, 1986), a child's initial production and comprehension of a linguistic form are mediated by a representation that is not accessible to reflection. Because he cannot reflect on one form's relation to another, his use of a form cannot be influenced by rules about such relations; it is simply shaped by positive and negative feedback from adults. Once "procedural success" is achieved (i.e., once he consistently uses the form correctly), its representation will become accessible to unconscious reflection or to what Karmiloff-Smith calls "metaprocedural operators." According to Karmiloff-Smith (1986, pp. 107–108), these operators scan representations and are

> sensitive to identical forms paired with different functions and to identical functions paired with different forms. A process is then initiated such that . . . representational links are established and defined explicitly. . . . The computational load caused by metaprocedural operations often makes it necessary for the child to mark externally, i.e., behaviorally, the new links which have become defined internally. This behavioral marking acts, in my view, as a form of "cognitive processing prop," rather like the role of linguistic scaffolding in social interaction, of overt rehearsal in memory, of finger counting, and so forth.

The chief virtue of this account is that it explains why some errors in the use of related forms occur only after a considerable period of correct use.

For example, Bowerman (1978, 1982) reported that her daughter began to use "put" mistakenly in contexts in which "give" was more appropriate even though she had been using both verbs correctly for weeks. According to Karmiloff-Smith, these errors cannot occur before links between the representations of the verbs have been established by metaprocedural operations. Karmiloff-Smith (1979) herself also reported cases in which French children began to add a partitive incorrectly to expressions of number—for example, saying "un de mouchoir" (one of handkerchief) instead of "un mouchoir" (one handkerchief)—even though they had previously used only correct expressions. According to her theory, this error cannot occur until the dual functions of "un"—for expressing either number or nonspecific reference—are made explicit by metaprocedures. Once this occurs, the child creates a difference in form ("un de" versus "un") to "externally mark" the difference in function.

Although she does not address the issue of ME, Karmiloff-Smith's theory is incompatible with the claim that children keep the extensions of a new word and an old from overlapping. Children cannot impose ME between two extensions unless they have explicitly linked their representations, and such links will be established only after words have been used correctly for some time. The theory can accommodate only the claim that children make the extensions of two old words mutually exclusive.

Karmiloff-Smith's proposal that metaprocedures are sensitive to cases in which two forms have common functions, and that a functional difference may be temporarily created to "behaviorally mark" a difference in form, could be taken to imply that children will impose ME between two old words that have common referents. However, the matter is unclear because she does not specify the amount of functional overlap that is necessary to compel children to create temporary functional differences. Children may "behaviorally mark" the difference between two words that share a few referents by imposing ME, or they may react this way only if two words share all referents.

Finally, from Bowerman's (1978, 1982) evidence of late-emerging confusions, which Karmiloff-Smith interprets as supporting her theory, it is clear that the children began to violate ME by using pairs of verbs for common referents even though they had previously maintained ME between them. In other words, Karmiloff-Smith's theory can accommodate evidence for the delayed onset of ME violation, so its compatibility with any kind of ME claim is not great.

SUMMARY

If children were biased to construct mutually exclusive extensions, their word learning would be profoundly affected. The bias could influence their decisions about the reference of ambiguous words (disambiguation), about the need to reinterpret old words (correction), about the acceptability of new words (rejection), and about the appropriateness of generalizing words to new referents (restriction).

Although the bias is potentially very powerful, its relation to behavior is complex, if not slippery. To maintain ME, a child must show the restriction effect but need show only one of the other three effects; moreover, she might still fail to show any of the effects in some situations. Because the bias is not an absolute constraint, it can be overridden: in some situations, the child may receive convincing evidence that two words have referents in common; in others, she may violate ME rather than give up some more strongly held belief. It is also possible that some children have the bias but do not impose ME until they have had sufficient experience with a particular pair of words.

Theorists who have explicitly addressed the issue of an ME bias have advocated one of three views—that children have it from the beginning of word learning, that they never have it, or that they acquire it during the preschool years. In support of the first view, Barrett (1978) argued that, without the bias, words would remain hopelessly overextended. We countered that only eventually do children need to impose ME between some words in order to correct overextensions; because they do not always need to contrast, they might not need an ME bias, at least not during early childhood. Markman (1984) claimed that adherence to an ME principle promotes the construction of maximally useful extensions. We raised the objection that, in some situations, a child might actually have to abandon the most useful kind of extension—a basic-level category—to maintain ME. Clark (1983a) proposed that a desire to avoid lexical gaps may be the motivation for the bias; however, we noted that the bias would only prompt children to fill same- rather than different-level gaps rather than to avoid gaps entirely. Other arguments have focused on why younger children should be more likely to have the bias than older ones. The bias would seem to suit younger children better because the vast majority of their words are supposed to be mutually exclusive; the same is not true for older children. Also, younger children may have cognitive limitations that prevent or impede their construction of overlapping extensions. Refutations of these arguments were presented.

Both Gathercole (1987) and Nelson (1988) have advanced the second view—that children never have the bias. Both cite numerous studies in which children have been observed to accept two names for the same thing. However, this finding by itself does not discredit the ME hypothesis: children could have a strong bias, yet overcome it in certain situations. Gathercole's other arguments were found to be more damaging to Barrett's and Clark's theories than to the ME hypothesis itself. Finally, both Gathercole and Nelson proposed that the child language phenomena accounted for by an ME bias could be explained in terms of input and preexisting concepts. We noted inadequacies in these explanations.

Finally, several arguments have been offered in support of the view that the bias develops during the preschool years. First, because of cognitive limitations, young children may not think about a thing's membership in one category when considering whether it belongs to another (Merriman, 1986b); an implication of this argument is that method of questioning may affect whether young children show an ME bias. Second, young children might try to simplify the problem of coordinating two names for the same thing by giving the names identical interpretations. Third, children may not induce a general ME rule until they have had enough experiences in which the correction of an old name and the introduction of a related new one co-occur (Merriman, 1986). Fourth, according to Mervis (1987), the bias will not develop until children accept adults' authority on categorization issues. However, we countered that such acceptance is only a prerequisite for the correction effect, not the ME bias. Finally, we presented several arguments for why young children might not need the bias and for why older children might be helped by a kind of "default option" ME bias.

The general theories of Karmiloff-Smith (1986) and MacWhinney (1987) were discussed because, although neither explicitly addresses the ME hypothesis, they do bear on it. According to MacWhinney, children sense conflict when two words seem to have referents in common. Although extensions are not revised immediately, ME is eventually imposed if the words are never heard for the same referent. According to Karmiloff-Smith, children will allow two forms to have identical functions but eventually alter the functions of one or both so as to establish a one-to-one form-function relation. This argument could be applied to the ME issue by proposing that children allow two words to have common referents but eventually alter the meanings of one or both so as to preserve ME. Neither Karmiloff-Smith's nor MacWhinney's theory supports the prediction that children will react to hearing a new word for an old word's referent by immediately imposing ME.

Several important theoretical issues have been considered—namely, the bias's potential effects on word learning, its relation to development, its interaction with other beliefs and biases, and its prerequisites (cognitive, attitudinal, and experiential). However, we have neglected two very important issues—those of nature-nurture and of metalinguistic representation—because theorists have tended to ignore them.

Although those who have argued that the bias is present from the beginning of word learning have not expressly claimed that it is innate, it is difficult to think of prelinguistic "nurture" experiences that would instill it. On the other hand, the view that the bias emerges during the preschool years is not necessarily a nurture position. Although delay in the development of the bias could be due to insufficient nurture (e.g., not receiving enough of a certain kind of linguistic input), it could also be due to insufficient maturation, or to both. Expression of the bias may depend on the development of certain skills (e.g., the ability to monitor the relation between extensions) that may have a strong maturational component. Thus, ME could be a late-emerging but innate principle—one that is not accessed until children develop both the ability to think about extensional relations and the tendency to do so spontaneously.

In Karmiloff-Smith's (1986) and MacWhinney's (1987) theories, both nature and nurture affect the expression of the bias. Innateness in MacWhinney's account is reflected in the postulated response to words that are used for similar referents—activation of competition processes and increased sensitivity to distinguishing data. Nurture plays a role, however, because patterns of name input ultimately determine how the competition between words is resolved, that is, whether ME is imposed. In our application of Karmiloff-Smith's theory to the issue, the child is endowed with a natural tendency to impose ME between words that have been used for common referents. However, ME will not be imposed until nurture "indicates" that procedural success has been achieved, that is, until feedback from adults about the words is consistently positive.

Theorists have not specified whether the bias is an aspect of metalinguistic knowledge, that is, whether children are aware of how it affects their lexical processing. Children might try to impose ME between words but not realize that this is what they are trying to do or correct an old word in response to the introduction of a new one but not justify their action in terms of ME. No theorist has addressed whether children would ever express the ME principle with a statement such as, "It can't be both a cat and a raccoon," or how the bias might affect definitions of related words or responses to such metalinguistic questions as, "Is a raccoon a kind of cat?" Even Markman (1984, 1987), who characterizes ME as an assumption that children make, does not address the issue of their consciousness of their own assumption.

II. EMPIRICAL STATUS OF THE BIAS

The major issue that divides the theoretical treatments we reviewed is the question of developmental change. Several theorists have proposed that the bias is present from the beginning of word learning (Barrett, 1986; Clark, 1987; Markman, 1987), but others have argued that it does not develop until the preschool years (Merriman, 1986b; Mervis, 1987). We first review the evidence concerning toddlers and then that concerning older children.

TODDLERS

Three kinds of data are available for evaluating the nature of the bias in toddlers—parents' diaries, tests of naturally acquired words, and tests of either unfamiliar or recently trained words. These three kinds of data represent different points along a continuum in which naturalness declines as experimental control increases.

Diaries of Spontaneous Production

The diary data are useful for documenting instances of ME violation, that is, cases in which a toddler produces more than one name for the same referent. Those who have analyzed the data have assumed that, if such instances are rarely observed, then toddlers probably have an ME bias. However, for reasons discussed in the previous chapter, this assumption is questionable. A nonbiased child might avoid ME violations if he were conservative in word generalization and rarely heard names for similar referents; in contrast, a biased child might produce numerous ones if he tended to delay imposing ME until he acquired a certain amount of knowledge about word pairs. Diary data are suited for evaluating only the "immediate" versions of the correction and restriction effects. The former is produced if something is removed from the extension of an old word as soon as it becomes part of a new word's extension and the latter if two words are never used for the same referent. However, even these uses of diary data are problematic. We will survey specific diary analyses one by one and then delineate their general limitations.

Clark's review.—Clark (1973) presented data from several diary studies in composite form to illustrate how children's overextension of animal names tends to subside as new names are learned. She noted one instance of ME violation—for a short time, one child used two names interchangeably for new animals. Clark also characterized Pavlovitch's (1920) data as showing how a French child narrowed the extension of "bebe" (baby) as new words were acquired. These data also contained one ME violation—the child referred to herself by both her proper name and "bebe." Finally, Clark discussed data from Leopold (1949) that showed how a child restricted the extension of a vehicle name as she learned new vehicle names. Here too Clark noted violation—the child used two terms to refer to cars for a period of 3 weeks. Clark's summaries thus indicate that temporary overlaps of extension do occur as new words are acquired but that their occurrence is infrequent.

Clark (1973) also noted that a general decline in overextensions seems to occur at the same time as an accelerated growth in vocabulary. Although she did not explicitly argue that this co-occurrence was evidence for an immediate correction effect, it might be so construed. One could argue that overextensions decline because the ME bias compels children to restrict old word extensions to "make room" for those of many new words. However, Clark did not conduct within-diary correlational analyses to substantiate her impression, and subsequent diary analyses cast doubt on it. In a longitudinal study of six toddlers, McShane (1980) observed that only three showed a surge in vocabulary growth; moreover, this surge began around the age of 18 months, which is a full year prior to the time that Clark estimates that the general decline in overextensions occurs. In another diary analysis, Rescorla (1976, 1980) found that the percentage of words overextended by six children (24%–29%) was stable from their fifteenth to their twentieth month, a period during which a surge in vocabulary growth occurred for some. Furthermore, if one considers absolute numbers rather than percentages, the overextension tendencies of this sample increased both during and after the surge.

Barrett's analysis of Leopold's diaries.—Barrett (1978) analyzed Leopold's (1939, 1949) records of the overextensions produced by the latter's daughter between her first and second birthdays. The aim of the analysis was to evaluate the central prediction of contrast theory—that specific overextensions cease once appropriate new names are acquired. The results are summarized in Table 1. Only one violation of the prediction was identified, and

TABLE 1

BARRETT'S (1978) SUMMARY OF THE OVEREXTENSIONS RECORDED BY LEOPOLD (1939, 1949)

Lexical Item	Initial and Subsequent Referents	More Appropriate Lexical Item
"pa"	Father/grandfather/mother (1-0); any man (1-2)	"Mama" (1-3) "Mann" (1-5)
"ann"	Pictures of adults (1-5); any adult (1-6)	"Frau" (1-7)
"by"	Self/other children (1-2)	"Boy" (1-8)
"y"	Any child (1-8)	...
"ll"	Balls (1-0); balloon/ball of yarn (1-4); observatory dome (1-8); balls of tin foil and paper (called "paper-ball")/marbles/ovoid ball (called "egg-ball")/a spherical bead (called "ball-beads") (1-11)	"Balloon" (1-10) "Beads" (1-9)
"ck-tock"	Square watch (0-11); other clocks and watches/round gas meter (1-0); fire hose wound on spool (1-2); bathroom scales (1-3); machine with disk-shaped dial (1-4); a round eraser (1-9)	...
"schentuch"	Handkerchief/napkin (1-10)	...
"bby pin"	A particular type of pin used in the child's hair/any shaped hairpin (1-7)	...
"h"	Locomotive game with toy bricks (1-0); real trains and cars/pictures of cars/toy wheelbarrow/old-fashioned carriages/riding motions (1-4)	"Auto" (1-5) "Choo-choo" (1-7) "Wheelbarrow" (1-11) "Ride" (1-8)
"to"	Pictures of cars (1-5); real cars (1-8); Bradyscope/airplane (called "piep-piep Auto," literally "bird car") (1-9); electric mangle (1-10)	"Airplane" (1-11)
"oo-choo"	Trains (1-7); Bradyscope (1-9); airplane/wheelbarrow (1-10); streetcar/a trunk (1-11)	"Airplane" (1-11) "Streetcar" (1-11) "Wheelbarrow" (1-11)
"heel"	A wheelbarrow wheel (1-8); a wheelbarrow (1-10); toy wagon/a ring (1-11)	"Wheelbarrow" (1-11)
"a]	Dogs (1-0); pictures of dogs (1-1); cows (1-2)	"Dog" (1-11)
"uwau"	Dogs (1-1); stone lion (1-1); horses (bronze book-ends)/toy dog/soft slippers with face (1-3); fur-clad man in poster (1-4); porcelain elephant (1-6); picture of sloth (1-8); cake lamb (1-9)	"Mann" (1-5) "Shoe" (1-6) "Cake" (1-9) "Hottey" (horse) (1-10) "Dog" (1-11)
"at"	Toy sailboat (1-10); airship (1-11)	...
""	Cod-liver oil (1-6); all other oily preparations used on child (1-6)	...
"k bottle"	Milk bottles (1-10); bottle containing white toothpowder (1-10)	...
"ke"	Candy (1-6); real cakes and sand cakes (1-9)	"Candy" (1-10)
"okie"	Cookies/crackers/cakes (1-6)	"Cracker" (1-7) "Cake" (1-6)
"ndy"	Candy (1-10); cherries/anything sweet (1-11)	...

NOTE.—Reproduced from Barrett (1978, pp. 210–211) by permission of the Cambridge University Press. The age of the child at the time of overextension and at the time of acquisition of the more appropriate word is given in parentheses in years and months.

that was questionable—the child created a novel compound in which the old word modified the new one ("ball-beads").

One might question the generality of the data because the child acquired language under atypical conditions—her father spoke mostly German and her mother mostly English. The bilingual nature of the input, however, makes the result only more persuasive as evidence for an ME bias. Multilingual input contains many more ME violations—that is, instances in which more than one name is used for the same referent—than monolingual input. It is very difficult to attribute a bilingual child's tendency to preserve ME to input rather than to a disposition.

However, Barrett's analysis missed nine instances of ME violation. Clark (1973) noted one in her review, that the child used two names for cars— "sch" from 1-0 to 1-6 and "Auto" from 1-5 on (Leopold, 1939, pp. 40, 121–122). Gathercole (1987) identified another:

"Doggie" [was first heard at] 1;11. A late synonym for "Wauwau" [which was used from] 1;3–2;0. "Dog" [first heard] 1;11 did not gain ground against these competitors. [Leopold, 1939, p. 78]

We found an additional seven:

The word "Auto" . . . was once applied at 1;8 to a toy duck on wheels, which was otherwise called "duck." [Leopold, 1949, p. 131]

"Hase" [German for "rabbit"] was used only this once for an Easter rabbit, a toy. She probably called it otherwise "Wauwau" or "dolly." [Leopold, 1939, p. 88]

But for some time she said it ["down"] only upon special request, whereas "up" was active and served also for the wish to get down in spontaneous utterances. [Leopold, 1939, p. 63]

On the third day of 1;3 she called her mother "mama." . . . Misuse of "papa" for her mother was corrected by the end of 1;3. [Leopold, 1939, p. 98]

At the end of 1;8 the word ["Frau"] finally appeared spontaneously. . . . At the middle of 1;11 she repeatedly said "Mann-Frau" for woman, which proved that "Frau" was not yet detached from "Mann" in her subconscious mind. In fact, she still used "Mann" for woman at 2;1. [Leopold, 1949, p. 131]

Operating the light switch was a fascinating experience. She said "light out" at 1;8, and "aus" [German for "out"] in the same situation 1;10. She used "an," from the German presentation "Licht an," at 1;10 correctly, but also for the opposite operation, switching the light off. . . .

either word could be used as a signal for operating the switch. [Leopold, 1949, pp. 144–145]

"Miau" served as [the term for "cat" from] 1;8–2;1. But on May 27, 1932 [1;10], we got a kitten for her. At first referred to it as "Miau," also called it "kitty, kitty" with falsetto voice. [Leopold, 1939, p. 70]

Barrett's analysis is subject to other criticisms as well. First, the test of his central prediction is not as compelling as it seems because the child did not learn a correct alternative for eight of the 20 overextended words before her second birthday (see Table 1). As Gathercole (1987) has argued, some factor other than an ME bias must be responsible for the correction of these words, and it may also account for the correction of the other 12 as well. This argument assumes that the child actually corrected the eight words during the period of the study. One piece of evidence that supports it is that nearly all specific overextensions of these words are entered only once in the diary (see Table 1); for example, she called a round gas meter "tick-tock" at 1-0 but was never heard to make this mistake again, despite never learning an appropriate name for gas meter. Thus, Barrett's finding may be an artifact of the child's general tendency to maintain specific overextensions for only short periods. Second, as Barrett acknowledged, it was impossible to evaluate two cases in which an overextended and correct word were used in the same month because Leopold had not reported precise dates for their use. We discovered another indeterminate case: at 1-4, the child called pictures of children "Bild" (German for "picture") and "baby" (Leopold, 1939, p. 52). Finally, there was a substantial base rate tendency for any word use (not just an overextension) to cease during the period of study. Leopold (1939, p. 159) reports that, "of the 377 words which had been used, 136, or 36%, were inactive by 1;11."

In addition to examining diaries to determine whether an overextension ever overlaps with a correct extension, one can also check whether two correct extensions ever overlap. Admittedly, in the latter case, input might contradict ME; that is, two correct words may be heard for the same thing (e.g., "sofa" and "couch"). However, if the ME bias were an especially strong one, such overlaps might be resisted. Other word learning dispositions have been shown to be sufficiently strong to cause resistance to contradictory input. For example, Katz et al. (1974) found that toddlers' disposition to generalize names for inanimate objects was so strong that they ignored a cue indicating that a name was not to be generalized—after hearing "This is Zav" in reference to a wooden block, they generalized the name to other blocks.

Leopold's daughter was quite willing to allow correct extensions to overlap. Because her input was bilingual, two kinds of correct overlapping extensions were possible—those involving words from the same language and those involving words from different languages (translational equivalents). The former were rare because, as already noted, the vast majority of words in monolingual input to a toddler have mutually exclusive extensions. Gathercole (1987) did identify one case—the child used both "boy" and "baby" for boys (Leopold, 1939, p. 52). We found two more examples— "baby," "Hilde," and "I" (which usually took the form "my") were used for self-reference (Leopold, 1939, pp. 34, 87) and "Haus" and "Bau" (German for "house" and "building," respectively) for the same structures (Leopold, 1939, p. 90). In contrast, Hilde used over 30 pairs of translational equivalents (most of these are listed in Leopold, 1939, pp. 177–179; Gathercole, 1987, cited seven of these cases). This finding challenges not only the claim that Hilde had an ME bias but also Clark's (1987) claim that bilingual toddlers generally resist learning the translational equivalents of familiar words. One could argue that Hilde permitted these bilingual overlaps because she knew that the words belonged to different languages—that she maintained ME only within a language. However, Leopold (1939, 1949) concluded that his daughter had not yet realized that she was dealing with two languages: she mixed German and English within phrase boundaries, did not tend to respond in the language in which she was addressed, and even coined a few words by blending German and English. Thus, numerous ME violations can be found in what was a one-language system for the child.

Other diaries.—It may be that bilingual input presents so many ME violations that it destroys a child's natural ME bias. The bias may stand a better chance under conditions of monolingual input—especially if that input consists primarily of mutually exclusive basic-level words. Unfortunately, available diaries of monolingual toddlers do not approach the exhaustiveness of Leopold's records.

Barrett (1978) found support for his central prediction in Lewis's (1951) observations of a child's acquisition of animal terms. The child stopped calling dogs, cows, and cats "ti" once he started naming these animals correctly and stopped applying "ti" to horses one day after he started calling them "horse." He also stopped overextending "horse" to large dogs once he learned to call them "dog." However, one can find other passages in Lewis's book (e.g., pp. 121, 128) that do not support Barrett's prediction:

> When K. was able to repeat "cakie" in imitation, he still used "e e" when he desired cake. In certain situations, the child will revert to the old word.
>
> K. had many names for coconut or snow.

Also, the child's base rate for discontinuing specific overextensions cannot be estimated from Lewis's report.

Barrett (1982) analyzed the speech of two children who had been observed periodically for 9 months during their second year. One overextended nine words and never violated ME; the other overextended 13 and violated it only once, calling Barrett "Mummy" even though she knew his name. Barrett argued that this was not a true violation because "Mummy" was used in this instance not as a name but as a request for action. However, Gathercole (1987) noted that one of the children did allow "baby" and "girl" to overlap. Also, because correct alternatives were never learned for 12 of the 22 overextended words, only 10 words could be analyzed for conformity to Barrett's prediction. Finally, there was a considerable tendency for overextensions to decline even when correct alternatives were not learned. Most specific overextensions were recorded only once; for example, a child called a toy truck "bus" for the first time at 1-8, but this mistake was never observed again despite the fact that "truck" was not acquired during the period of the study.

Barrett (1986) noted several apparent violations of ME in the speech of his 1-year-old son Adam but presented the following three arguments to discount them. First, he proposed that not all Adam's one-word utterances were acts of naming. For instance, when Adam said "chuff-chuff"—his term for train—on seeing a railway bridge even though he knew "bridge," Barrett argues that the child was not really calling the bridge a train; rather, seeing the bridge just made him think of trains. The problem here is lack of any evidence regarding the child's intention. Although the name was produced in the presence of a thematically related object (something a train goes over) rather than a taxonomically related one (another vehicle), Adam may have intended to name; his noun extensions may have included thematic associates. Bauer and Mandler's (1989) finding that 1-year-olds tend to extend names taxonomically rather than thematically could be taken to support Barrett's argument. However, their study showed only that taxonomic associates are preferred over thematic ones, not that thematic associates are excluded. A child could allow both—just as children allow both typical and atypical referents despite a preference for the former (Kuczaj, 1982).

Second, other apparent violations are to be discounted, according to Barrett, because they are processing errors. Thus, Adam called a donkey "horse" even though he knew "donkey" either because it looked to him more like a horse than a donkey or because he accidentally retrieved the wrong word (i.e., he did not say what he meant to say). The problem here is the same as previously—there is no evidence for deciding between alternative explanations. Barrett argued that the fact that Adam adopted the correct name when his incorrect name was challenged supports the processing error explanation. But would a child who believed both names to be correct have responded to such a challenge any differently?

Finally, Barrett argued that Adam occasionally engaged in willful misnaming, calling something by the wrong name while laughing or smiling and refusing to respond to requests that he produce the correct name. Here too alternative explanation cannot be ruled out. Adam's refusal to produce the correct name may have reflected his belief that the word he was using was correct, or he may have laughed and smiled simply because he enjoyed being defiant.

Evidence of children's failure to produce the immediate correction and restriction effects can be gleaned from other monolingual diary evidence as well. Gathercole (1987) has cited reports of one child using color words indiscriminately during his second year (Cruse, 1977), of children as old as 7 years using "many" and "much" interchangeably (Gathercole, 1979), and of children using modified adjectives "X-er," "too X," and "X-est" interchangeably with "X" and "very X" (Clark, 1980; Gathercole, 1979). Mervis (1987), who kept detailed notes of her son's production and comprehension of "duckie" from the time he was 10 months old, reported that he learned to produce names such as "goose," "ostrich," and "pelican" for different categories of bird but still occasionally called all these "duckie."

A final source of disconfirming diary evidence concerns children's indiscriminate production of morphological variants of the same word. Ruke-Dravina (1959) observed a Latvian child's indiscriminate use of nominative and accusative noun forms, plural and singular noun forms, and masculine and feminine adjective forms. Brown (1973) reported the indiscriminate use of plural and singular nouns by American children. Finally, Kuczaj (1977) noted that children tended to use correct irregular past tense verb forms (e.g., "went") at the same time that they used overregularized forms (e.g., "goed," "wented"). One could argue that the immediate restriction and correction effects should not be expected for pairs of words that children can identify as having a common root; however, this argument does not defend the hypothesis against Kuczaj's result since some regular and irregular forms do not have the same surface root.

General limitations.—A number of weaknesses limit the use of diary data for detecting ME violations. As Clark (1973) noted, most diarists pay more attention to the point at which a child starts using a word than to when she stops doing so. Note, for instance, that in her diary study Rescorla (1976, p. 163) instructed mothers, "Whenever you notice that your child understands something new, try to jot it down on the record form." No matter how dedicated the diarist, a substantial proportion of a child's utterances are likely to be missed (Merriman, 1986a), and the goal of keeping up with the appearance and disappearance of every word becomes increasingly difficult as the child's acquisition of vocabulary accelerates. Leopold (1939) indicated that the goal was not feasible beyond his daughter's second birthday; Rescorla's (1976) mothers began to fall short of the goal at an even earlier point. Thus, diary analyses are of little use in tracking ME violations by children aged 2 years or older.

Another weakness is that diarists do not systematically record parents' reaction to overextension. Although parents will tolerate some overextensions (Mervis & Mervis, 1982), they are likely to correct others. Leopold (1939) and his wife frequently corrected their daughter for calling women "Mann." Barrett's (1986) remarks about how he and his wife responded to their son's apparent processing errors and willful misnamings suggest a vigilance against overextensions. Finally, Lucariello and Nelson (1986) reported that a sample of 10 mothers had a .76 probability of immediately rejecting the overextensions that their 2-year-olds produced in natural settings. Thus, overextension may cease before a child learns a correct alternative name, not because the child has an ME bias, but because parents have successfully corrected the overextension (Gathercole, 1987).

A final weakness is that diarists record instances of word comprehension only rarely. This is critical for three reasons. First, a young child typically comprehends a word several months before producing it (Benedict, 1979; Goldin-Meadow, Seligman, & Gelman, 1976). There may be a period during which she comprehends a new word but continues to overextend another word to its referents in both production and comprehension; by the time the new word is produced, she may have corrected the overextension. Second, as already discussed, the child may produce a word without intending to name (Barrett, 1982). Barrett indicated that comprehension tests can be used to distinguish such pseudo-overextensions from the real thing; presumably, if she had been asked, "Where is Mummy?" the girl who had called Barrett "Mummy" would have ignored Barrett and searched for her mother. Third, a child could stop producing a word either because she believes it is wrong or because she merely prefers to use another word, and comprehension data could be used to decide between these explanations. Arguments derived from both basic-level theory (Mervis & Rosch, 1981) and competition theory (MacWhinney, 1987) for why a child might prefer to use a new word over an old one even if both were believed to be correct were presented earlier.

Tests of Naturally Acquired Words

This kind of evidence has one of the same limitations as the diaries—namely, the influence of input is indeterminate. If a child maintains ME between two words in a test of her extensions, this may be due to her parents having used the words for very dissimilar referents or to their having explicitly corrected one word as they introduced the other (e.g., "That's a spoon, not a fork"). Nevertheless, such evidence has some utility because adults should maintain ME in the input they provide about certain words (e.g., "spoon" and "fork") but violate it in input about others (e.g., "spoons" and "silverware"). Cases in which children violate ME when input is likely to have maintained it should count against the claim that they have a strong bias, and cases in which they maintain it even though it is violated in input should have the opposite import.

Cases in which ME is maintained in input.—Rescorla (1976) conducted monthly tests of six children's comprehension and production of nouns from three semantic fields—animals, vehicles, and fruits. These tests began around each child's first birthday and ended 6–8 months later. The test data were supplemented by maternal diaries and monthly interviews in which mothers were asked about their children's vocabulary. In an exhaustive appendix, Rescorla described the extension of every noun from the three fields by every child in every testing session. There were 62 instances in which a noun was overextended and the correct noun for the referent was subsequently learned; in only seven instances did the overextension stop once the correct noun was acquired.

This result is quite discrepant with Barrett's (1978) finding that productive overextensions tend to cease once correct names are produced. One reason for the discrepancy may be Rescorla's (1976) use of comprehension data. Thirty of the ME violations in her corpus are cases in which one name was overextended in production to something that could be identified correctly only in comprehension. For example, a child called a bus "truck," never produced "bus," but comprehended "bus." One could argue that children knowingly misapplied the old name in such cases because they could not retrieve or articulate the correct name and so used the closest "produceable" word; they do not really believe that something can have two names. The main problem for this argument is that 25 ME violations involved productive overextensions that persisted after the correct name could be produced. (For additional criticism of this argument as an explanation of every overextension, see Merriman, 1986a.) The prevalence of such violations is corroborated by Thomson and Chapman's (1977) finding that, in 16% of the cases in which a 2-year-old named a picture incorrectly, the child had used the correct name for some other picture during the test session.

Mervis and colleagues (Mervis & Canada, 1981, 1983; Mervis & Mervis, 1982) conducted periodic tests over a 9-month period of three toddlers' production and comprehension. The test set consisted of toy kittens, cars, and balls; things that looked like kittens, cars, and balls; and other toys. After playing with the toys, the children were asked to name each one and then tested for comprehension of "kitty," "car," "ball," and every other word they had used for the toys. Mervis (1984) replicated this design with 12 toddlers, half of whom had Down syndrome. Both studies showed that the toddlers did not stop overextending old names in either production or comprehension after correct names were acquired in comprehension. For example, in the replication study, an overextension persisted for at least one test session after the correct alternative had been acquired in 95% of the cases.

These studies indicate that, contrary to Barrett's (1978) prediction, toddlers do not tend to correct overextensions as soon as appropriate new names are acquired. However, the studies do not necessarily indicate that toddlers lack an ME bias. They could have one but express it by rejecting or disambiguating new names rather than by correcting old names. Also, they could delay the imposition of ME until they have acquired sufficient knowledge about a word pair. Unfortunately, the data are of little use in evaluating these possibilities.

One could argue that, because toddlers do allow some new names to share referents with old ones, they would probably not reject or disambiguate new names. However, Mervis (1984, 1987; Mervis & Canada, 1981) has presented evidence from both diaries and tests that shows that toddlers occasionally have to be "persuaded" to accept a new name for an old name's referent. Mervis and Canada (1981, p. 5) noted that, when mothers simply present a new name, "the children often demonstrate immediate rejection of the new label, either by making the object function as though it was still a member of the child-basic category, or by labelling it with the child-basic name." The children accepted new names in such cases only if their attention was drawn to a distinctive object property. For example, if a toddler called a round candle "ball," he tended to resist the suggestion that it was called "candle" unless his attention was drawn to its wick or its waxy texture.

Cases in which ME is violated in input.—There have been two investigations of toddlers' interpretation of naturally acquired, non–mutually exclusive words; both have assessed the interpretation of basic-level/superordinate noun pairs by children older than 24 months. Callanan and Markman (1982) found that both 32- and 41-month-olds showed some tendency to transform superordinate nouns into collective ones, that is, to interpret nouns such as "toy" and "child" the way adults interpret names such as "pile" and "team." They were more likely to reject a superordinate noun for an individual (e.g., "Is this a toy?") than for a group (e.g., "Are these toys?"). This pattern of response would be appropriate for collective nouns, which are names for groups, not individual items. The children were also more likely to select a group as the referent of the singular form of the superordinate noun (e.g., "Give me a toy") than to select an individual as the referent of its plural form (e.g., "Give me toys"). They did not show similar tendencies for basic-level nouns such as "ball" and "girl." Callanan and Markman argued that, although superordinate nouns were less likely to be misinterpreted than to be interpreted correctly (24% vs. 76% of the trials), the results indicate that toddlers find it easier, or somehow better, to think of the superordinate/basic-level relation as that between a collection and a class rather than as that between two classes. Callanan and Markman argued that the fact that collection errors were made at all is significant because they conflict with syntactic cues that are present when superordinates are introduced and because collective nouns rarely occur in input to children.

Macnamara (1982, chap. 5) obtained evidence of a stronger collection misinterpretation tendency in somewhat younger children—28-month-olds. On nearly half the test trials, the children denied that an individual item could be called "animal" or "toy." Most of these denials were accompanied by what Anglin (1977) terms the dominant name response (e.g., "No, piggie"). A second experiment showed that 95% of a sample of 29-month-olds accepted that a group of different animals could be called "animals" but that only 55% accepted that a group of dogs could be so called; a third experiment showed that 33% were unwilling to imitate sentences such as, "A pig is an animal."

Markman (1987) has suggested that an ME bias underlies the collection error. By deciding that a new superordinate noun refers to a group, children avoid having to accept that a single object can be called by both this noun and a familiar basic-level noun; thus, a specific instance of the disambiguation effect is produced. However, Macnamara (1986) has pointed out a flaw in this argument: if children really made a collection interpretation, they should also reject the plural form as a name for a single group. For example, one group of players is not to be called "teams" or one collection "piles." However, children accept plural superordinate nouns for single groups. According to Macnamara, this indicates that 2-year-olds interpret superordinates not as collective nouns but as class nouns that can be used only in the plural (similar to "clothes"). One could counter that, if this is true, an ME bias may still be the motivation for the error; however, this misinterpretation preserves ME only between names for individuals, not between those for groups. Although a shirt could not be called both "shirt" and "clothe," 10 shirts could be called "shirts" and "clothes." Callanan and Markman (1982) found that 32-month-olds were quite willing to violate ME between names for groups (e.g., to accept that a pair of horses could be called both "horses" and "animals"), but Macnamara (1982) found that 28-month-olds were not. Children may be willing to violate ME between names for groups before they do so between names for individuals. If this is so, it begs explanation.

Another argument against Markman's proposal that an ME bias causes superordinate misinterpretations is that the latter could be the simple result of the way adults use superordinate nouns in speech to children (Gathercole, 1987; Macnamara, 1986). Adults tend to use them only in reference to heterogeneous groups (Callanan, 1985; Shipley et al., 1983; White, 1982) and even occasionally model the collective misinterpretation (Callanan, 1985). Thus, it may be incorrect to construe misinterpretations as instances in which ME is imposed despite input that violates it. Also, if a homogeneous group is assumed to be more similar to a heterogeneous group than to an individual, this may account for why children appear to violate ME between names for groups before they violate it between names for individuals. A child who first hears "animal" applied to a heterogeneous group may be more willing to generalize the name to a homogeneous group of animals than to a single animal.

A final counterargument to Markman's proposal is that the tendency to reject superordinate nouns for either individuals or groups may have more to do with the difficulty of superordinate categorization than with an ME bias. As Rosch, Mervis, et al. (1976) have noted, superordinate classes have very little cohesiveness. Children may map a superordinate noun to a collection rather than a class because they cannot generate a cohesive class for it. Three- and 4-year-olds have difficulty in matching-to-sample problems that are based on superordinate categorization (Markman & Hutchinson, 1984; Rosch, Mervis, et al., 1976); they also have difficulty using superordinate nouns even when they do not know alternative basic-level names (Anglin, 1977). Furthermore, in an experiment in which a new name was introduced for something children had identified by an old name, Merriman (1986b) found that many 2½-year-olds allowed the names to overlap but that only 4% judged the new name to be superordinate to the old one, suggesting that, even when toddlers are not concerned to maintain ME, they may find it rather unnatural to construe a new name as superordinate to an old one.

Tests of Unfamiliar or Recently Trained Words

These tests provide the most information about the nature of the bias because they allow for careful control of input. They can be designed to compare the name correction tendencies of children who either do or do not learn a competing new word, and they also provide the only means for unconfounding the disambiguation, rejection, correction, and restriction effects. Their only potential drawback is unnaturalness: words may be presented in ways that are quite dissimilar to how they ordinarily are, and the results may not generalize to natural word learning.

Tests of the disambiguation effect.—Vincent-Smith, Bricker, and Bricker (1974) showed 22- and 29-month-olds several pairs of objects, each consisting of something the children could name (e.g., a truck) and something they could not (e.g., a spatula). For each pair, the children were asked to "Pick the X," where X was the name of the unfamiliar object. Both groups of children produced the disambiguation effect; that is, they tended to select the thing they could not name rather than the one they could. Golinkoff, Hirsh-Pasek,

Baduini, and Lavallee (1985) obtained similar results with 30-month-olds, using sets that contained one unfamiliar and many familiar objects.

There are two problems with these studies. First, as noted in the discussion of Merriman's (1986b) proposals, toddlers might pick an unfamiliar object simply because they are attracted by its novelty. This problem can be remedied either by showing that they would not pick it if they were simply asked to pick an object (see Markman & Wachtel, 1988) or by preexposing it so as to decrease its relative novelty (see Chap. III). Neither of these remedies were tried. Second, in both studies the children were corrected whenever they selected the familiar object; this corrective feedback could have taught them to pick the unfamiliar object.

Even if the toddlers' performance in these studies is not an artifact, only the weakest ME bias is needed to produce the disambiguation effect. A stronger bias is required for the other effects; it must be strong enough to compel correction of belief about an old name, or rejection of someone's use of a new name, or resistance to the temptation to generalize a name to something similar to known referents. In tests of the disambiguation effect, there seem to be no other biases or beliefs that might conflict with the ME bias: a child who must choose between a spatula and a truck does not have to resist some natural inclination to map "spatula" to truck.

A final consideration is that the disambiguation effect could be produced by a bias to fill lexical gaps (Clark, 1983a) rather than by an ME bias. A child might select an unfamiliar over a familiar object, not because he wants to avoid having two names for the same thing, but because he wants to avoid having no name for something. Adults would probably pick unfamiliar objects in the test of the disambiguation effect (Markman & Wachtel, 1988), but they might not necessarily consider mutually exclusive extensions to be preferable to overlapping ones. Thus, although the individual must disambiguate, reject, or correct to maintain ME between a new and familiar names, the production of one of these effects could be motivated by something other than an ME bias.

Tests of the immediate correction effect.—In several studies, toddlers have been trained to give a new name to the referent of an old one and then tested for whether they correct the latter. These studies are similar to those of naturally acquired words in indicating that toddlers do not show an immediate correction effect.

Nelson and Bonvillian (1973) attempted to teach 16 new object names to 16-month-olds over a 6-month period. The children tended to overextend old names to the training objects throughout the study, and 34% of these overextensions were to objects that they had also learned to name correctly. This percentage is even higher if one counts cases in which a child was heard to name objects correctly from the same category as the referent of an overextension. Although this result suggests a strong tendency to violate ME, this conclusion must remain tentative since the study lacked a control group of children who did not receive name training. If such a group showed a greater tendency to overextend old names, then this would give evidence of a limited restriction effect.

Oviatt (1980) successfully trained 15–17-month-olds to comprehend both a noun ("rabbit") and a verb ("press it"). She found that, in violation of ME, some also produced old names for the referents of the trained names. However, just as in Nelson and Bonvillian's (1973) study, there was no control condition.

Banigan and Mervis (1988) taught 24-month-olds six new nouns. Each referred to something the children had called by an old name in a pretest (e.g., those who had called a unicorn "horse" were taught "unicorn"). Instructions varied (e.g., a distinctive property of the referent might be described), but explicit information about the new name–old name relation was not conveyed. After training, production and comprehension tests were administered. The test objects were not identical to those used in pretest and training but came from the same categories (e.g., a different unicorn was used). In 96% of the instances in which the referent of a trained name was correctly selected, the same object was also selected as a referent of the old name. These results are nearly identical to those Mervis (1984) obtained in her longitudinal study of naturally acquired words. Although this study lacked a control group, the rate of ME violation was so high that it would have been nearly impossible for control children to have overextended the old names any more frequently.

Merriman (1986b) conducted a name-training study different from the others in that both an "old" and a new name were trained within a period of 10 min. In this study, 2½-year-olds (as well as older children—see the next section) were taught an artificial name for a novel object; for example, they learned that a styrofoam ball with an attached sponge was called a "pilson." After training, they were asked to indicate whether any of several other objects had this name. Later, a second name (e.g., "tukey") was introduced for one of the objects that they had selected. There were two control conditions; one differed from the experimental condition in that the second name was introduced for an object the children had not selected, and the other differed in that children were told that the two names were mutually exclusive (e.g., "This is a tukey, not a pilson"). Comprehension of both names was tested. Those who heard the second name used for an object they had called by the first name showed no tendency to select mutually exclusive extensions. Their tendency to correct the first name was slight and no greater than that of the control children who heard the second name used for an object that was outside the first name's extension.

Merriman's (1986b) argument that toddlers violate ME because they are unable to coordinate concepts was supported by the performance of the control children who received explicit ME input. Four of the 12 children selected the object they had been told was "a tukey, not a pilson," as a referent of both names; two others allowed the names to share other referents, and only six maintained complete ME. If those who violated ME understood the explicit input and were willing to accommodate it, then only a failure to coordinate concepts can explain their violation.

Tests of the immediate rejection effect.—Banigan and Mervis (1988) compared the effectiveness of various ways of introducing a new name for an old name's referent. The 24-month-olds were much more likely to acquire the name if a distinctive property of the referent was highlighted in input both verbally and gesturally than if it was highlighted only verbally, only gesturally, or not at all. Although this finding supports Mervis's (1987) claim that toddlers will reject a new name for an old referent unless their attention is drawn to a distinctive property, an alternative explanation can be advanced—namely, that highlighting a distinctive property merely makes an object and its name easier to remember. Jacoby and Craik (1979) have argued that memory retrieval depends to a great extent on how distinctively an item has been encoded.

One limitation of Banigan and Mervis's (1988) study is that a name generalization test was used to measure name learning; that is, the correct test objects were similar but not identical to the training objects. In a study in which distinctive object properties were not highlighted, Taylor and Gelman (1988) found that 2-year-olds were more likely to resist generalizing a new name when it had been trained for the referent of an old name. Thus, Banigan and Mervis's test may have underestimated the word learning of the children whose attention had not been drawn to a distinctive property. In fact, Banigan and Mervis reported that many of these toddlers responded to test instructions by ignoring the test objects and searching for the original training object, suggesting that they had learned the name but had assigned a very restricted extension to it.

Taylor and Gelman's (1988) results are also problematic for Merriman's (1986b) proposal that inability to coordinate concepts is responsible for toddlers' tendency to violate ME. At least some of the toddlers in Taylor and Gelman's study were capable of coordinating interpretations of two names—otherwise there would have been no effect of old name knowledge on name generalization. The key word may be "some," however. In Merriman's (1986b) study, six of the control children who received explicit ME input coordinated interpretations of the two names, but the remaining six did not; Taylor and Gelman's result could be due to the responses of a similar portion of their sample. However, some explanation is needed for why no 2-year-old in the experimental conditions of Merriman's study reinterpreted one name in response to the introduction of another. There are at least three viable hypotheses. First, more processing capacity may be required to coordinate interpretation of a new name with a reinterpretation, rather than a fixed interpretation, of an old one. Second, toddlers may resist reinterpreting an old name either because they are reluctant to admit that they misinterpreted it or, as Mervis (1987) has argued, because they do not accept adults' authority as namers. Finally, toddlers may lack an ME bias but possess Clark's (1987) brand of contrast disposition. All these hypotheses would accommodate the apparent discrepancy between Taylor and Gelman's and Merriman's results.

Summary

The diary evidence does not offer strong support for claims that toddlers avoid ME violation. Reanalysis of Leopold's (1939, 1949) records of his daughter's speech reveals nine counterexamples to Barrett's (1978) claim that a name was never overextended to something that could be named correctly; moreover, the child tended to correct specific overextensions even when she did not learn appropriate names. Additionally, she used over 30 pairs of English and German equivalents despite lacking awareness that these were from different languages. Violations could also be found in the diary records of monolingual children's speech. Perhaps the most telling point, however, is that numerous violations were detected despite the fact that diary analysis is biased against such detections.

Like the diary evidence, the test results indicated that toddlers frequently allow naturally acquired basic-level names to share referents. However, they may occasionally reject new names that are introduced for old names' referents, especially if their attention is not drawn to distinctive properties. This result supports Mervis's (1987) argument that young children show the rejection rather than the correction effect. Also, they show a disambiguation effect with respect to new superordinate nouns, such as "animal" and "toy." They initially restrict these to heterogeneous groups, then extend them to groups that can also be denoted by familiar names, and finally apply them to individual referents of such names. It is unclear whether this developmental pattern merely reflects aspects of input or the difficulties of superordinate classification or whether it also reflects the mediation of an ME bias.

The evidence from tests of unfamiliar or recently trained words converges with the other sources in showing that, although toddlers do not show the immediate correction effect, they do produce some of the other ME effects. Some 2-year-olds fail to immediately correct even when an old name is explicitly corrected as a new name is introduced—a result that supports Merriman's (1986b) proposal that an inability to coordinate concepts underlies this failure. Two-year-olds do show the disambiguation effect; that is, they tend to select things they cannot name, rather than ones they can, as the referents of unfamiliar names. However, this behavior could reflect a novelty preference or a bias to fill lexical gaps rather than an ME bias. The results of one name-training study (Banigan & Mervis, 1988) have supported Mervis's contention that toddlers will show the rejection effect when their attention is not drawn to distinctive properties. However, an alternative memory-enhancement explanation for this finding cannot be ruled out, and the extent to which measures reflected learning rather than generalization is unclear. No training study has used measures of overt resistance (e.g., the child saying, "No," when a new name is introduced) to assess the rejection effect, although such resistance has been noted in some diary analyses and tests of naturally acquired words.

There are too few data and too many theoretical possibilities for a firm conclusion to be reached about whether toddlers have an ME bias. Those who would argue for a limited bias can point to the evidence of disambiguation and rejection effects. Those who would argue against it can find support in three findings—that words are frequently allowed to share referents (contrary to the restriction effect), that the introduction of a new word rarely prompts the correction of an old one (contrary to the correction effect), and that the rejection effect does not occur when attention is drawn to distinctive properties. Either side could generate explanations to discount the evidence of the other. Most of the arguments we have discussed are for the no-ME-bias position; however, the following is an example of how the pro-ME-bias position could be salvaged. Assume that toddlers have three competing biases—to maintain ME, to fill lexical gaps (i.e., seek names for salient categories), and to maintain interpretations of old names. Their failure to show an immediate correction effect could be due to their ME bias being weaker than their bias to maintain interpretations. Their failure to reject new names for distinctive referents of old ones could be explained by their ME bias being weaker than their bias to fill lexical gaps. Their tendency to disambiguate could be attributed to both the ME and the gap-filling bias. Finally, their rejection of new names for nondistinctive referents could be caused by their ME bias. Whether this or many other possible accounts is valid cannot be determined from the available evidence; however, whatever the account, the facts indicate that toddlers have at most a weak ME bias.

OLDER CHILDREN

The evidence concerning the ME bias in older children is drawn from tests of either naturally acquired or unfamiliar/recently trained words.

Tests of Naturally Acquired Words

Cases in which ME is maintained in input.—Although several investigations have examined whether toddlers select mutually exclusive extensions for basic-level nouns, no study has addressed this question for older children; however, there have been studies of older children's extensions for relational words, and these reveal considerable ME violation. The many studies that Clark (1973) marshaled in support of her prediction that children would initially interpret antonyms as synonyms constitute a strong empirical challenge to the ME hypothesis for older children; interpreting a pair of antonyms as synonyms (e.g., "big" and "small" as both meaning big) is tantamount to violating ME with respect to every referent of the pair. Ironically, these studies also present a challenge to Clark's (1987) own view that children never believe that any two words are synonyms.

Consider three defenses of the ME hypothesis against this evidence. First, not all studies supported Clark's prediction (for a thorough review, see Richards, 1979). Nevertheless, regardless of how many studies failed to support it, those that did must count against the ME hypothesis, unless they can be dismissed on other grounds. Moreover, some of the studies that failed to uphold Clark's prediction revealed other kinds of incorrect synonymies. For example, Bartlett (1976) and Brewer and Stone (1975) found that children tend to interpret adjectives of the same polarity, such as "big" and "high," as synonyms, and Kuczaj (1975) found similar misinterpretations of "always" and "never."

A second defense is to argue that children who appear to interpret a pair of antonyms as synonyms actually have no knowledge of one or both terms; they merely adopt a consistent way of responding to commands containing them. For example, Carey (1978) found that children respond to a request to "make it so I have ——— tea" the same way regardless of whether "less," "more," or "tiv" is used—they add tea. The problem for this defense is that a child with a strong ME bias should not respond to an unfamiliar word in the same way as to a familiar one; he should show the disambiguation effect. If he knows what "more" means and hears, "Make it so I have tiv tea," he should do something other than add tea.

One could counterargue that children become flustered when given unfamiliar requests or that they are so set to respond in a certain way (e.g., by adding tea) that they do not listen carefully. However, in many studies alternative responses were readily available. For example, in Donaldson and Wales's (1970) study, some children selected the same stick as both the longest and the shortest even though there were many other sticks they could have picked. Also, children have been observed to give the same response to two nonsynonymous words while reacting differently to a nonsense word (Brewer & Stone, 1975). Third, incorrect synonymies are often evident in production; for example, Gathercole (1979) observed children to use "much" and "many" indiscriminately, and Richards (1976) reported the same for 5-year-olds' use of "bring" and "take." Finally, children sometimes justify their misinterpretation of an adjective in terms of another one. Ravn and Gelman (1984) found that many children who incorrectly picked the taller but smaller of two rectangles when asked to "pick the big one" justified their selection by saying, "Because it's taller." Kuczaj and Lederberg (1977) observed the same phenomenon in children who interpreted "younger"/"older" as meaning "shorter"/"taller."

The final and best way to defend the ME hypothesis against this evidence is to point out that violations can occur even if children have the bias because other biases or beliefs counteract it. Also, only a portion of a child sample is typically found to interpret antonyms as synonyms; it could well be that the remainder have been guided by an ME bias to avoid overlapping extension. The kind of study that would be most useful—one that would compare children who know a word to those who do not for their interpretation of its antonym—has not yet been reported. Even if some children who know "before" interpreted "after" as meaning prior to, for example, the ME hypothesis would be supported if more of those who did not know "before" interpreted "after" this way.

Cases in which ME is violated in input.—Investigations have focused on two types of cases—that of the relation between superordinate and basic-level nouns and that of the relation between pairs of nouns that have both common and unique referents.

Anglin (1977) observed that preschoolers occasionally reject superordinate nouns such as "animal," "food," and "plant" as names for individual items. These rejections are usually accompanied by the "dominant name response" (e.g., "That's a person, not an animal"), and the effect is similar to the one Callanan and Markman (1982) and Macnamara (1982) have observed in toddlers. Anglin noted that such rejections were inconsistent—rarely was a superordinate name rejected for all the things that could be labeled by familiar names—and that referents were rejected only when they were both atypical and familiar. For example, "animal" tended to be accepted as a name for cow (typical and familiar), anteater (typical and unfamiliar), and centipede (atypical and unfamiliar) but not for butterfly (atypical and familiar). Anglin attributed this familiarity effect for atypical instances to the greater likelihood that children knew specific names for the familiar than for the unfamiliar referents, which is essentially an argument that an ME bias was responsible for the rejections. This argument can be challenged, however. Although posttests determined that the children were better able to name the familiar than the unfamiliar atypicals, those who could name a specific atypical were not more likely to reject it than those who could not. That is, although more children knew "butterfly" than "centipede," those who knew "centipede" were no less likely than those who did not to accept that a centipede can be called "animal."

Even if Anglin's explanation is correct, the implication is that the ME bias has only a limited effect on decisions about name extension. Knowledge of basic-level names did not interfere with the extension of superordinate names to typical examples and only partially interfered with that to atypicals. Also, the results of Callanan and Markman's (1982) study, which included a group of 3½-year-olds, indicate that preschoolers are quite willing to violate ME by mapping both a superordinate and a basic-level noun to a homogeneous group.

Some pairs of terms belong to different semantic systems for subdividing the same general category: for example, names for religious identity (e.g., "Catholic," "Jew") and for nationality (e.g., "American," "Lithuanian") subdivide the set of all people in different ways. Because the systems' criteria for subdivision are different, many cross-system pairs have both common and unique referents: some but not all Jews are American, and some but not all Americans are Jews. Children have some tendency to make such cross-system pairs mutually exclusive. Elkind (1961) found that 74% of Jewish 6-year-olds judged that a person could not be both a Jew and an American, but only 10% of Jewish 8-year-olds thought so. He reported (Elkind, 1962) a similar trend for Catholic children's judgment of the possibility of being a Catholic and an American. An ME bias might underlie the 6-year-olds' mistake; indeed, when asked to justify his judgment, one child cited the ME principle: "You can't have two." Elkind noted that this mistake was rarely made by children who could list at least one characteristic of their religion that distinguished it from others (e.g., "A Jew goes to Temple"). There is a striking analogy between this and Mervis's (1987) finding that toddlers will resist a new name for an old name's referent unless they perceive it to have a distinctive property.

Sigel, Saltz, and Roskind (1967) found that 60% of 6-year-olds judged that a father who goes to work as a doctor is no longer a father, but only 20% of 8-year-olds thought so. However, 60% of 8-year-olds thought that a father who became a drunkard was no longer a father. These findings may have more to do with children's mistaken notions of what a father is than with an ME bias. Several studies of kin terms (Chambers & Tavuchis, 1976; Haviland & Clark, 1974; Piaget, 1928) have documented that 6- and 8-year-olds consider characteristic actions and appearances rather than blood relationships to be essential to the meanings of these terms. This may also explain why 6-year-olds judge that two kin terms cannot apply to the same person (Chambers & Tavuchis, 1976; Haviland & Clark, 1974; Piaget, 1928).

MONOGRAPHS

Tests of Unfamiliar or Recently Trained Words

Tests of unfamiliar or recently trained words have provided data relevant to three issues—whether older children show the disambiguation effect, whether they produce the immediate correction effect, and whether they tend to misinterpret input that violates ME. There have been no tests of the immediate rejection effect in older children.

Tests of the disambiguation effect.—Dockrell and Campbell (1986) conducted three studies of the disambiguation effect in 3- and 4-year-olds. The first was rather serendipitous. Children were taught to call a tapir "patas" and a week later were asked to pick out the patas from a set containing a tapir, a pig, a cow, and a sheep. Nearly all the children performed correctly; however, so did nearly all the subjects in a control condition, who did not receive the name training. The tapir was the only unfamiliar kind of animal in the test set. Similar results were obtained in the second study, in which a new fruit term was trained. The third study demonstrated how the disambiguation effect can hinder word learning. Seven children were told to "Pass the *gombe* block, not the red one or the green one, but the gombe one." All inferred that the experimenter was referring to a silvery hexagonal block rather than to a red cube or a green square. Two weeks later, when asked to find "gombe ones," four responded as if "gombe" meant hexagonal, two as if it meant silvery, and one as if it meant either hexagonal or silvery. Dockrell and Campbell argued that the children who misinterpreted "gombe" as a shape rather than a color name probably did so because silvery was already part of the extension of a familiar name (e.g., "blue") but hexagonal was not. Unfortunately, pretests to determine the extensions of children's color and shape names were not conducted. Also, all three studies had the same problems as investigations of the disambiguation effect with toddlers—either novelty preference or a bias to fill lexical gaps, rather than the ME bias, could have produced their results.

Markman and Wachtel (1988) conducted the best tests of the disambiguation effect to date. In their study 1, 3- and 4-year-olds were shown pairs that consisted of an object they could name and one they could not. Half the children were asked, "Show me the X," where X was an artificial name, and the remainder were asked, "Show me one." The latter group served as a control for novelty preference. The former group selected the objects they could not name on 82% of the trials, which was significantly greater than chance, whereas the control group selected them on only 55% of the trials. Thus, the novelty preference explanation could be ruled out. However, as already noted, a disposition to fill lexical gaps rather than one to preserve ME could account for the disambiguation effect. Also, the fact that children erred on 18% of the trials requires explanation. These trials may have simply been instances of child inattention or uncooperativeness, or they could reflect true individual differences in one or both of the biases.

Markman and Wachtel (1988) also examined another variant of the disambiguation effect. They argued that, when a new noun is introduced, it may refer to a whole object or to some attribute (e.g., color, substance, a part); because of their categorical relations bias—the belief that common nouns designate categories of whole objects—children assume that a new noun refers to a whole object. However, if they already know a name for the whole object but not for a salient attribute, the ME and categorical relations biases come into conflict. Results supported this conceptual analysis. In studies 2 and 3, 3-year-olds were much more likely to interpret a new noun as a name for a prominent part if they already knew a name for the whole object (71% vs. 26% of the trials); in studies 4–6, a similar effect was obtained for substance interpretations. The results of all five studies, however, could be explained in terms of a bias to fill lexical gaps rather than an ME bias. Nevertheless, the studies demonstrate that the ME or the gap-filling bias can override as well as be overridden by the categorical relations bias.

Tests of the immediate correction effect.—In a study by Carey and Bartlett (1978), preschoolers were told to get "the chromium tray, not the blue one," in reference to two trays—one olive and the other blue. They were later tested for whether they had learned that "chromium" is a name for olive and, if so, whether its extension overlapped with that of familiar color words (e.g., "green"). A very weak immediate correction effect was obtained. Only nine of the 19 children retained any information about "chromium," and, of these, only two decided that it was the only name for olive, that is, reinterpreted the old color name by removing olive from its extension. Two decided that "chromium" and "green" were synonyms and another two that "chromium" and "green" had overlapping extensions; for the remaining three, the status of "chromium" was unclear. Thus, the children were actually more likely to violate ME than to maintain it. However, the findings do suggest that the introduction of a new word can compel a few children to restrict the extension of an old word, although the study lacked a control group to verify that no children would have done so spontaneously. If preschoolers have a weak ME disposition, it can clearly lose out when placed in competition with other beliefs (in this instance, the correct belief that "green" is an acceptable name for olive).

Unlike the 2½-year-olds in Merriman's (1986b) successive name-training experiment, 4- and 6-year-olds showed the immediate correction effect. Forty-two percent of the 4- and 69% of the 6-year-olds removed an object from a name's extension after a second name was introduced for it; the age-related difference was significant. Control groups showed no tendency to revise a name extension when a second name was introduced for an object outside it. This study is the only one to compare the size of the immediate correction effect in different age groups.

Merriman's (1986b) results also support the claim that the ME bias can be counteracted by implicitly contradictory input. In one condition of his experiment, the same object property was emphasized when both names were taught; in others, either no property or unique properties were stressed. Subjects in the first condition were least likely to impose ME (33% vs. 74%), and those in the other two conditions did not differ. One might have expected children for whom unique properties were emphasized to have been more likely to maintain ME than those in the no property condition. The finding of a nonsignificant difference is actually more compatible with the notion of ME as the default relation: input that implicitly signals ME (e.g., emphasis on unique properties) should not make children more likely to impose ME because they should already be highly likely to do so. In fact, 11 of the 12 6-year-olds in the no property condition posited an ME relation.

Gathercole (1987) has noted that Harris's (1975) classic studies of 5–7-year-olds' ability to infer the properties of new words indicated that there are limitations on older children's ME bias. In one experiment, the children were told that an "X is a Y," where X was an artificial word (e.g., "mib") and Y was either bird, flower, man, or drink, and then asked, "Is X a Z?" where Z was a subordinate of Y (e.g., "A mib is a bird. Is a mib a robin?"). The children said "yes" slightly less than half the time, in violation of ME. In a second experiment, 10 of 12 children who were told, "Mib is a white drink," responded affirmatively to, "Is mib milk?" Thus, ME interpretations were made less frequently by the children in these studies than by the 6-year-olds in the no property and unique property conditions of Merriman's (1986b) experiment. However, the high number of ME violations that resulted when "mib" was described as a "white drink" is quite compatible with Merriman's finding that emphasis on a common property prompts children to allow names to share referents.

The greater number of ME violations in Harris's (1975) than in Merriman's (1986b) study may reflect differences in the extent to which input at both training and test signaled violation. Non-ME relations were made more salient in the instructions used by Harris. First, children were told that a new name A shares all its referents with the familiar name B and then asked about A's relation to the familiar name C, which was known to share all its referents with B. This kind of questioning could very well create an *atmosphere effect* (Begg & Denny, 1969)—because the two known relations among the three terms are overlapping, children may be disposed to interpret the remaining relation as such. Second, the question form, "Is A a C?" presupposes that it is reasonable to consider A's to be C's, which may make children more likely to judge that they are.

Markman and Hutchinson (1984, experiment 2) also found a high level of ME violation by 4–5-year-olds. The children were shown a picture of a familiar thing (a cow) and told it was "a kind of X," where X was an unfamiliar name. When asked, "What do you think X means?" 54% answered with a familiar name, and the rest gave descriptions. Like the studies of Harris (1975) and Merriman (1986b), these results indicate that, if preschoolers have an ME bias, its expression is often preempted by other beliefs and interpretative strategies.

Tests of whether input violating ME will be misinterpreted.—The only test of this prediction is also the only name-training experiment involving children beyond the age of 7 years. Markman, Horton, and McLanahan (1980) had 6-, 11-, 14-, and 17-year-olds learn three artificial names—one for each of two sets of unfamiliar objects and one for the combined sets. The sets were constructed to be analogous to two related basic-level categories, such as shirts and shoes. Names were introduced for groups (e.g., "These are fims"), and subjects were tested for whether they applied them to individual items. The only name judged to be inapplicable was the one that had been introduced for the combined sets, that is, the superordinate name, and only the three youngest groups made this mistake. These results are thus analogous to those of Callanan and Markman's (1982) and Macnamara's (1982) studies, in which 2- and 3-year-olds were observed to reject naturally acquired superordinate names for individuals. Unfortunately, one of the alternative explanations we offered for these studies is also appropriate here—namely, the results may reflect children's difficulty in abstracting superordinate categories rather than their resistance to ME violation. Also, even if an ME bias is responsible, errors were made only on approximately half the trials; that is, ME was maintained in many cases. Thus, the conflict between preserving ME and interpreting input correctly was not always resolved in favor of the former. Finally, when children were told in training that the basic-level names were each a "kind of" the superordinate name, they showed very little tendency to reject the latter. This result is also consistent with the view that ME is a default relation that can be overridden by contradictory input.

Summary

The evidence for the existence of an ME bias is much stronger for older children than it is for toddlers. First, two studies have shown that some older children react to the introduction of a new name for an old name's referent by immediately correcting the old name. This evidence is problematic for theories such as Karmiloff-Smith's (1986) and MacWhinney's (1987) that are not compatible with ME being imposed immediately after a name is introduced. It also presents a challenge to the proposals by Clark (1987) and

Markman and Wachtel (1988) that after toddlerhood the ME bias grows weaker or disappears. Merriman (1986b) actually found the immediate correction effect to be stronger in 6- than in 4-year-olds.

Second, the evidence concerning older children's rejection of superordinate names for individuals, although not completely convincing, implies the ME bias much more strongly than the findings for toddlers. Anglin's (1977) results suggest that older children are more likely to reject such a name for an individual if they already know the basic-level name for it. Markman et al.'s (1980) results indicate that older children tend to reject trained superordinate names for individuals even when syntactic information in input is incompatible with such a reaction. Because this evidence was obtained via immediate testing, it also challenges the argument that children will impose ME only after a delay.

Finally, the results of studies of the disambiguation effect in older children imply the ME bias more strongly than do those performed on toddlers. Markman and Wachtel's (1988) first study clearly rules out the novelty preference explanation for 3- and 4-year-olds' tendency to map a new name to a new rather than an old referent. These authors also demonstrated that disambiguation can occur even when it conflicts with children's categorical relations bias.

Although the research indicates that older children have the ME bias, it also shows that the bias has limited strength. Their tendency to immediately correct old nouns can be checked by input that only implicitly contradicts ME. They often interpret relational words that should be mutually exclusive as if these had identical extensions. They nearly always allow the extensions of naturally acquired superordinate names to overlap with basic-level ones when referents are typical and even occasionally when they are not. When told that one new name "is a kind of" another, they interpret the first as subordinate to the second.

If ME is the default option in older children's procedures for relating new to old names (as we proposed in Chap. I), then they should not adhere to the ME principle consistently; their tendency to adhere should be inversely related to the strength of other contradictory beliefs. The data generally fit this prescription. Older children showed the greatest adherence in Markman and Wachtel's (1988) study 1, in which there were no other factors that might have prevented them from selecting a new over an old kind as the referent of a new name. Their adherence was weakest either when input explicitly contradicted ME or when ME could have been maintained by rejecting an old name for something they were quite confident it named, such as a typical example. In other situations (e.g., when the bias conflicted with the categorical relations bias), they showed a moderate tendency to maintain ME, indicating that, although the bias can be counteracted by a competing belief, it is not so weak as always to lose out in such competitions.

Although the findings suggest that the ME bias grows stronger over the first 6 years of life, research has been somewhat biased against toddlers. Some of the best studies, such as Markman and Wachtel's (1988) and Markman et al.'s (1980), which were designed so as to rule out alternative explanations, have not involved toddlers. It is therefore appropriate to conclude only that children do not show an immediate correction effect until sometime after their third birthday. This developmental trend need not reflect the delayed acquisition of an ME bias; it could, for example, result from a developmental increase in willingness to accept adult authority (Mervis, 1987). More research in which the performances of toddlers and older children are compared is needed; we report studies of this kind in the remaining chapters.

III. EXPERIMENT 1: DISAMBIGUATION BY YOUNG CHILDREN

Merriman (1986b) derived his claim that the ME bias develops during early childhood from the results of his study of the immediate correction effect; however, there are many reasons why toddlers might not show this effect even if they had the bias. The purpose of our experiment was to compare toddlers to preschoolers in a task that should be affected by the bias, namely, deciding whether an unfamiliar name applies to something they can already name (an old kind) or something they cannot (a new kind). Subjects who have the bias should show the disambiguation effect by selecting the new kind.

There have been a few studies of the disambiguation effect (Dockrell & Campbell, 1986; Golinkoff et al., 1985; Markman & Wachtel, 1988; Vincent-Smith et al., 1974), but none of these has compared toddlers to preschoolers. Also, none except Markman and Wachtel's study (1988) has included the control condition necessary to unconfound a novelty preference from an ME bias explanation. According to the former, children select new kinds over old simply because new things are more attractive.

The procedure we adopted was similar to that used by Vincent-Smith et al. (1974), except that wrong answers were not corrected during testing, the children were asked whether they were familiar with each new name tested, and they were preexposed to referents of some of the new names. The last procedure was intended to reduce the novelty and hence the attractiveness of these referents. This control for novelty differed from that of Markman and Wachtel (1988), who tested an additional group of children for whether they would pick new kinds over old when asked simply to pick one. Our control had the advantage of being within subjects but the disadvantage of possibly not reducing attractiveness sufficiently; that is, even though children were preexposed to new kinds, they might still find these more attractive than old ones. We evaluated this possibility by comparing performance with new kinds that had been preexposed (new kind–old tokens) to that with ones that had not (new kind–new tokens).

The reason for asking children whether they were familiar with each new name was to determine whether the tendency to identify a new name as being new would be related to the disambiguation effect. We hypothesized that development of the former would precede or at least co-occur with that of the latter; we reasoned that, if a new name was not identified as new, it would probably not be consistently assigned to a new rather than an old kind.

METHOD

Subjects

The sample consisted of three groups of 12 children aged, respectively, 2 years (M = 2-0, range = 1-10–2-3), 3 years (M = 3-0, range = 2-10–3-3), and 4 years (M = 4-0, range = 3-9–4-3). There were equal numbers of boys and girls in every age group. One 2- and one 3-year-old were replaced because they failed to cooperate. The children, who came from middle-class homes, were located through published birth records.

Materials

Twenty-four objects judged to have names that children under age 5 years would not know (new kinds) and eight objects judged to have names that such children would know (old kinds) were collected; published norms were used to guide these judgments (Goldin-Meadow et al., 1976; Nelson, 1973; Vincent-Smith et al., 1974). The new kinds were divided into three sets; all objects are listed in Table 2. There were also three reserve new kinds—a spatula, pliers, and a funnel.

TABLE 2
TEST OBJECTS USED IN EXPERIMENT 1

New Kinds			
Set A	Set B	Set C	Old Kinds
Allen wrench	Cartridge	Binoculars	Ball
Binder clip	Cork screw	Casing	Car
Embroidery hoop	Cube	Clamp	Cup
Lens	Ducting	Garlic press	Doll
Plectrum	Gauge	Hinge	Key
Pump	Hole puncher	Party favor	Phone
Spiral	Magnifier	Scouring pad	Shoe
Tuning fork	Tweezers	Strainer	Spoon

NOTE.—In case children were familiar with "fork" or "puncher," the tuning fork was referred to as a "tuner" and the hole puncher as a "holer."

MONOGRAPHS

Procedure

Each child was tested individually in a lab room by a male experimenter. After establishing rapport, the experimenter placed one of the sets of new kinds on a table; selection of a particular set (A, B, or C) was counterbalanced within every age group. The child was encouraged to play with the objects for 5 min. The experimenter occasionally demonstrated how a particular object could be used but for the most part did not intervene. If the child happened spontaneously to name one of the objects correctly, the experimenter replaced it with a reserve object. These objects constituted the set of new kind–old tokens: the children did not know their names but became familiar with the objects during the preexposure period.

After play, the child was shown 16 pairs of objects—four instances of four kinds of pairs:

1. *New kind–old token versus old kind–new token (N-O vs. O-N).*—One of the new kinds from the preexposure set and an object the child had never seen before but should have been able to name (e.g., a tuning fork and a toy car).
2. *New kind–new token versus old kind–new token (N-N vs. O-N).*—Two objects the child had never seen before, only one of which could be named (e.g., a clamp and a toy car).
3. *New kind–new token versus new kind–new token (N-N vs. N-N).*—Two objects the child had never seen before, neither of which could be named (e.g., a clamp and a corkscrew).
4. *New kind–old token versus new kind–new token (N-O vs. N-N).*—Two objects the child could not name, one of which was from the preexposure set (e.g., a tuning fork and a corkscrew).

We use the phrase "never seen before" in the descriptions of the first two pairs only in reference to the object tokens; although the child may have had some familiarity with the object kind, it was assumed that the token was novel (e.g., the particular toy car was one she had never seen before). The pairs were presented in random order. The child was first asked, "Do you know what an X is?" Then the pair was presented, and she was asked, "Which one is an X? Put your finger on the X," where X was the name for the new kind and should thus have been unfamiliar. In the pairs listed above under 3, the new kind named was randomly selected, and, in those listed under 4, it was the name of the new kind–old token. For every pair, the correct object occurred as often on the left as on the right. (One object in each pair can clearly be designated as "correct" because it was the legitimate referent of the unfamiliar but real name.) The experimenter recorded the child's response to the first question as well as the object the child selected.

On all trials involving old kinds, after the child had selected an object, the experimenter picked up the old kind and asked either, "What is this?" or, if the child had just selected this object in the test, "What's another name for this?" This procedure was followed to ensure that the child could name the old kind (i.e., that it was indeed an old kind for the child). The entire procedure was administered in less than 15 min.

RESULTS

The percentages of correct selections for each kind of pair and each age group are summarized in Table 3. A 3 (age) × 4 (kind of pair) mixed analysis of variance of the number of correct selections yielded significant effects of age, $F(2,33) = 11.27$, $p < .01$, kind of pair, $F(3,99) = 18.45$, $p < .01$, and age × kind of pair, $F(6,99) = 4.16$, $p < .01$. Correct selections increased with age. All paired comparisons of age groups were significantly different by a Newman-Keuls test, $p < .01$. The kind of pair in which correct selections most frequently occurred was N-N versus O-N, followed by N-O versus O-N, then N-N versus N-N, and finally N-O versus N-N. All paired comparisons of the kinds of pairs were significantly different by a Newman-Keuls test, $p < .05$, except for the comparison of N-O versus O-N and N-N versus N-N, $p = .06$. The poorer performance on N-O versus O-N relative to N-N versus O-N pairs indicates that the children were less likely to select a new kind over an old when they had been preexposed to the new kind.

Because the interaction was significant, a separate three-factor (age) one-way analysis of variance was performed on the number of correct selections for each kind of pair. The age effect was significant only for N-O versus O-N pairs, $F(2,33) = 12.83$, $p < .01$, and N-N versus O-N pairs, $F(2,33) = 6.96$, $p < .01$. To compare these two age effects, a 3 (age) × 2 (kind of pair) mixed analysis of variance was performed on the number of correct selections in these two instances. Although marginal, the interaction was not significant, $F(2,33) = 2.63$, $p = .09$. The performance of 3- and 4-

TABLE 3

Selections of the Correct Referent of a New Name

Age	New Kind–Old Token[a] vs. Old Kind–New Token	New Kind–New Token[a] vs. Old Kind–New Token	New Kind–New Token[a] vs. New Kind–New Token	New Kind–Old Token[a] vs. New Kind–New Token
2-0	29	60	46	34
3-0	67	71	56	31
4-0	92	96	52	38

Note.—Entries are percentages based on four selections per subject, 12 subjects per age group.
[a] The correct referent.

year-olds on these two kinds of pairs did not differ significantly, but the performance of the 2-year-olds was significantly worse on N-O versus O-N pairs, $t(11) = 2.52, p < .05$.

Performance on each kind of pair was compared to chance level (50% correct). For N-O versus N-N pairs, the frequency of correct selections was significantly below chance, $t(35) = 3.59, p < .01$; each age group tended to pick a new token (i.e., one that had not been preexposed) when they did not know names for either object. Performance on N-N versus N-N pairs did not differ from chance; this result was also replicated when each age group's performance on these pairs was analyzed separately. This finding validates the crucial assumption that the new names were indeed unfamiliar to all the children. On N-O versus O-N and N-N versus O-N pairs, the 4-year-olds performed nearly perfectly. The 3-year-olds' performance exceeded chance on N-N versus O-N pairs, $t(11) = 2.42, p < .05$, but not on N-O versus O-N pairs, $t(11) = 1.51, p > .10$. Their performance on the latter pairs was bimodal; six chose correctly on 100% of the trials, whereas the other six chose correctly on only 33%. The 2-year-olds' performance did not exceed chance on N-N versus O-N pairs, $t(11) = 1.33, p > .10$, but was significantly below chance on N-O versus O-N pairs, $t(11) = 2.27, p < .05$.

The assumption that the children knew the names for the old kinds was supported. The 2-year-olds produced the correct name for them on 84% of trials, and both the 3- and the 4-year-olds did so on over 96% of the trials. If only those trials in which the children produced the correct names for the old kinds are analyzed, the results are unchanged; in fact, the 2-year-olds' scores change by less than 1%.

Older children were more likely than younger ones to acknowledge that a new name was unfamiliar. A three-factor (age) one-way analysis of variance of the number of "no" responses to the question, "Do you know what an X is?" in which X was an unfamiliar name, yielded a significant age effect, $F(2,33) = 7.39, p < .01$. The mean percentage of "no" responses was 6%, 36%, and 63% for the 2-, 3-, and 4-year-olds, respectively. Individuals tended to answer "no" either to nearly all or to nearly none of the questions. Four 3-year-olds and seven 4-year-olds answered "no" to at least 14 of 16 questions; the remainder of these two groups answered "no" to only 1.8 questions on average. The 2-year-olds were more likely than the other groups simply not to answer; six of them answered at most only one of the 16 questions; in contrast, the others tended to answer "yes" ($M = 13.67$). Only two 3-year-olds and one 4-year-old failed to answer more than one question.

Both the tendency to show the disambiguation effect and the tendency to acknowledge that a new name was unfamiliar increased with age, but the latter lagged behind the former. This lag is seen most clearly in the performance of the 4-year-olds, who were near perfect in selecting new kinds over old but far from it in acknowledging the unfamiliarity of new names. However, disambiguation was not a strict precondition for acknowledgment of the unfamiliarity of new names. The four 3-year-olds who acknowledged such unfamiliarity of the new names on at least 14 of 16 questions did not perform any better on N-O versus O-N pairs than their age-mates. In fact, they chose correctly on only 50% of the trials, whereas the others did so on 75%. The significance of this difference cannot be assessed with such a small sample.

DISCUSSION

In two previous studies (Golinkoff et al., 1985; Vincent-Smith et al., 1974), toddlers showed the disambiguation effect; that is, they tended to map an unfamiliar name to a new kind rather than an old. This finding was not replicated in the present experiment. One procedure used in the other studies that could have produced this result artifactually—correction of mistakes on test trials—was not used. The fact that toddlers did not show a significant tendency to select a new kind over an old, even on pairs in which the new kind had not been preexposed, may be a consequence of this procedural change. The more significant outcome of the present study, however, is the demonstration that novelty biases toddlers' performance in tests of the disambiguation effect; the previous studies had not controlled for this bias. When the novelty of new kinds is reduced by preexposure, toddlers are more likely to select an old kind over a new as the referent of a new name. Even 3- and 4-year-olds' performance can be biased, though to a lesser degree, by such novelty. Only 4-year-olds consistently chose a new kind–old token over an old kind–new token, although half the 3-year-olds also did so.

The results of the present study are quite compatible with those of Markman and Wachtel (1988), the only other study to control for novelty preference. The 3½-year-olds ($M = 3$-8) in their study showed a disambiguation effect that was stronger than that of the 3-year-olds but weaker than that of the 4-year-olds in the present study. This convergence in results is remarkable in view of the methodological differences between the studies.

When added to those of Merriman's (1986b) study, the current results make a stronger case for the claim that the ME bias emerges sometime around the third birthday. However, the finding that all 4-year-olds show a reliable disambiguation effect is moderately discrepant with Merriman's earlier finding that only 53% of 4-year-olds showed the immediate correction effect. Also, the toddlers in that study—who showed no ME tendency—had a mean age of 2-9, which is only 3 months younger than the partially successful group of 3-year-olds in the present study.

The disambiguation effect may be a precondition for the immediate correction effect. The latter requires that an object be removed from the extension of an old name because a new name has been introduced for it. Subjects will make such a correction only if their ME bias is stronger than their belief that the object belongs in the extension of the old name and only if they are not inclined to choose some other strategy for preserving ME, such as rejecting or disambiguating the new name. They may also fail to correct if they do not perceive a distinctive property in the referent of the new name (Mervis, 1987). In contrast, none of these factors appear relevant to whether subjects show the disambiguation effect.

If there is very little to interfere with ME-biased children's production of the disambiguation effect, then they should select a new kind over an old on every trial. All but one of the 4-year-olds and half the 3-year-olds did so. This finding supports our claim that, once the ME bias emerges, it acts as the default option for integrating the extensions of new and old names. If there is no contradictory input or countervailing bias, children will assume that two names do not share referents.

As we noted in the previous chapter, a child who lacks the ME bias could nevertheless show the disambiguation effect. The entailment flows only in the reverse direction—a child who has the bias must show the effect. A child who lacks the bias but has a bias to fill lexical gaps (i.e., to make sure that new kinds get names; Clark, 1983b) must also show the effect. The 2-year-olds' failure to disambiguate thus implies the absence of both biases. The older children's production of the effect implies the presence of either one or both. One factor in favor of explanation in terms of an ME bias is parsimony; only this bias is sufficient to account for Merriman's (1986b) finding that most 4-year-olds showed the immediate correction effect.

Surprisingly, children did not always admit that new names were unfamiliar; for example, to the question, "Do you know what a garlic press is?" more than a few children answered "yes" with conviction. Although older children were more likely to acknowledge lack of familiarity, this developmental trend lagged behind the development of the disambiguation effect. Thus, our prediction that readiness to acknowledge that a new name is unfamiliar would be a necessary precondition for the disambiguation effect was not confirmed. We had reasoned that children would have to identify a new name as being new before they would reliably map it to a new kind rather than an old. There are several possible explanations for why our reasoning was faulty. First, children may not have conscious access to the processes by which they decide to map a new name to one kind rather than to another. As noted in the previous chapter, Karmiloff-Smith (1986) has argued that it is not uncommon for children's reflective processing of language to be initially unconscious. Those who disambiguated may have identified the new name as new at some unconscious level. Second, children's responses to questions about whether they know a name may not depend on whether a referent comes to mind when they hear the name; they may use some very weak criterion, such as whether the word merely sounds like a word they have heard before. Finally, their reluctance to admit that they do not know a word may just be an instance of a general reluctance to admit any kind of deficiency. For this last explanation to hold, however, 4-year-olds must be assumed to have less of this reluctance than younger children. We know of no independent evidence to support such an assumption.

Our finding of an age-related increase in the tendency to admit that a new name is unfamiliar bears resemblance to results from developmental studies of metamemory (Yussen & Levy, 1975) and comprehension monitoring (Markman, 1981) in which older, but not younger, children have been observed to acknowledge deficits in knowledge or ability. However, our finding differs in that the metacognitive cart comes after the cognitive horse—children who do not openly acknowledge that a new name is unfamiliar do reliably map it to a new kind rather than an old.

IV. EXPERIMENT 2: DISAMBIGUATION, IMMEDIATE CORRECTION, AND RESTRICTION BY YOUNG CHILDREN

Experiment 2 was designed to answer possible criticism of the first experiment as well as to generate data on the immediate correction and restriction effects.

An Improved Test of Disambiguation

One reasonable criticism of experiment 1 is that the 24-month-old subjects may have completely disregarded requests—when asked, "Which one is a garlic press?" for example, they may have simply grabbed for the more appealing object. It is thus possible that they believe that new names map to new kinds but that their strong desire to grab what appeals interfered with the expression of this belief. The same criticism extends to Vincent-Smith et al.'s (1974) study but not to the one by Golinkoff et al. (1985). In the latter, requests involving old and new names were intermixed; because the toddlers responded to both kinds of requests correctly, it cannot be argued that they simply picked the most novel objects. Note, however, that Golinkoff et al.'s study had other problems—no control for novelty preference and the possibility that explicit correction of incorrect responses quickly taught the children what response was expected.

A second criticism is that toddlers may have overextended old names to what we defined as new kinds. For example, suppose a toddler who was preexposed to a tweezers thought that it could be called "scissors." Later, when it was paired with an old kind (e.g., a shoe) and he was asked, "Which one is a tweezers?" he would have been choosing not between a new kind and an old but between two old kinds. For him, the tweezers is a token of an old kind—in his mind, it is a scissors. The critical issue is not whether something is actually a new kind but whether subjects believe it is since the disambiguation effect can be tested only by contrasting things that subjects think they can already name with those that they think they cannot. In experiment 1, it was established only that children did not know the correct names for the new kinds, not that they thought these were new kinds. If the toddlers had a strong tendency to extend old names to the new kinds, then the test of the disambiguation effect was not valid. This criticism also applies to the experiments by Golinkoff et al. (1985) and Vincent-Smith et al. (1974). Occasional overextensions were, in fact, produced in the preexposure period of the first experiment, but the experimenter did not systematically probe for these.

Experiment 2 was designed to address these criticisms. Pictures were used rather than objects so that children might be less inclined to grab the stimuli. Requests involving old and new names were intermixed during testing; if toddlers tend to ignore requests, their performance should be equally poor for both types of names. Finally, children were asked to name the new kinds during preexposure, and only those that they could not name were used in the disambiguation test, thus eliminating the problem created by children overextending old names to new kinds.

A Test of Immediate Correction

The present experiment included a trained name task—one in which a new noun is trained in reference to something believed to be a referent of an old noun—so as to test the hypothesis that children show the disambiguation before the immediate correction effect. This prediction follows from the assumption that, whereas there are no beliefs or biases that interfere with disambiguation, the same does not hold for immediate correction. A child who strongly believes that an old name applies to something may not be ready to abandon this belief when a new name is introduced for that thing. Also, immediate correction requires acceptance of the expert principle (Mervis, 1987) that adults "know best" when it comes to naming, and young children may not accept this dictum.

A second reason for including this test was to evaluate the generalizability of Merriman's (1986b) findings concerning immediate correction. He found that some children would immediately correct a name they had just recently been trained to use; here we focused on names children had acquired naturally and had probably used for months. Additionally, a between-subjects rather than a within-subjects measure of immediate correction was used; this difference might be important because the latter requires that children admit to an adult that they were wrong in having considered something to be a referent of a name, whereas the former does not. In the between-subjects design, some children are told a new name for an old name's referent, and some are not; the measure of immediate correction is the difference between the two groups' tendencies to accept the old name for it. It is actually not clear whether this indexes the immediate correction or the restriction effect; the distinction depends on whether children have decided that the old name applies to the referent before the new name is introduced, and this cannot be determined with this method. We nevertheless refer to it here as a measure of immediate correction in order to distinguish it from a clear measure of restriction that we also used (see the next section).

The trained name task was also designed to examine whether immediate correction would be mediated by object typicality. Children heard a new name for either a typical or an atypical referent of an old name; we expected that they would be less likely to immediately correct typical referents because they are more certain that these are correct and because they are less likely to perceive properties that distinguish these from other referents (Mervis & Rosch, 1981). The nondistinctiveness of typical referents makes it difficult to construct an extension for them that does not contain the other referents as well. For example, a child who is familiar with the name "doggie" and hears a collie called "collie" is unlikely to infer that it is wrong to call collies "doggie" because their resemblance to other animals she has learned to call "doggie" is too great—there is very little about collies that distinguishes them from other dogs. However, she might well make the opposite decision regarding a distinctive-looking dog, such as a chihuahua; because she is uncertain that it is a dog from the outset, learning that the new name "chihuahua" applies to it may convince her that it is not a dog. Anglin (1977, chap. 5) gave this sort of explanation for his finding that object familiarity inhibited preschoolers' acceptance of superordinate names only for atypical referents.

A Test of Restriction

Construction of a special kind of atypical referent allowed us to make a strong test of the restriction effect, that is, of aversion to generalizing a name to the referent of another name. Drawings were made of hybrid objects that possessed the properties of two familiar basic-level categories from the same semantic field, for example, a vehicle that has some properties of a truck (e.g., a squarish cab) and others of a car (e.g., four side windows). Although children should be inclined to extend two names to these hybrids, the ME bias should keep them from doing so. We also assessed children's tendency to extend two names to objects that were clearly typical of one name but atypical of the other.

A few studies (Mervis, 1984; Rescorla, 1976) have found that toddlers are quite willing to allow pairs of naturally acquired basic-level nouns to share referents, but no similar studies of older children have been conducted.

General Predictions

Based on Merriman's (1986b) hypothesis, we expected that children younger than 3 years would not show the disambiguation, immediate correction, or restriction effects. Also, on the basis of the hypothesis that the ME bias develops as a default option, we expected that the size of the effects for 3-year-olds would depend on the strength of countervailing beliefs and dispositions. The disambiguation effect should be the strongest because there are no obvious countervailing beliefs. As already discussed, several factors work against immediate correction. The primary potential hindrance to restriction is the disposition to generalize a common noun to referents that strongly resemble known referents (see Katz et al., 1974).

METHOD

Subjects

Three groups of 16 children, aged, respectively, 2 years (M = 2-1, range = 1-11–2-3), 2½ years (M = 2-8, range = 2-4–2-10), and 3½ years (M = 3-5, range = 3-0–3-11) served as subjects; seven 2- and three 2½-year-olds were replaced because their cooperation was lost before the procedure was completed. The two older age groups were selected to be younger than the corresponding groups in experiment 1 because the age of 36 months had been identified in that experiment as a point of transition and our intent was to test at ages either before or after this point. Additionally, age 2½ corresponds closely to that of the youngest subjects in Merriman's (1986b) experiment, allowing comparisons to be made with more confidence. As before, the children came from middle-class homes and were located through published birth records or by contacting local preschools and day-care centers; each group contained equal numbers of boys and girls.

Materials

For the disambiguation test, 50 colored drawings of objects were either composed by an artist or cut from picture books. The drawings were mounted on 5 × 7-inch cards; 31 drawings depicted objects that the children should have been able to name (old kinds), and 19 were of objects whose names they should not have known (new kinds). Each type of drawing was divided into two sets of roughly equal number; these are listed in Table 4. Selection of drawings was guided by published norms (Goldin-Meadow et al., 1976; Nelson, 1973; Vincent-Smith et al., 1974).

TABLE 4

Test Pictures Used in Experiment 2

Set 1		Set 2	
New Kinds	Old Kinds	New Kinds	Old Kinds
Cactus	Ball	Hoe	Apple
Feather	Bed	Mower	Balloon
Grill	Bird	Scale	Banana
Hydrant	Book	Screw	Bike
Igloo	Bunny	Skeleton	Bottle
Kite	Cake	Stethoscope	Chair
Octopus	Coat	Web	Comb
Pallette	Cow	Wrench	Flower
Shell	Cup		Horse
Swing	Dress		House
Wagon	Hat		Lamp
	Pants		Phone
	Pig		Shirt
	Spoon		Star
	Table		Television
	Tree		

An additional four sets of six colored drawings (either composed by an artist or cut from picture books) were used for the immediate correction and restriction tests. Set A consisted of two cars, two trucks, a hybrid car-truck, and a hand; set B included two spoons, two forks, a hybrid spoon-fork, and a fish; set C contained two crackers, two cookies, a hybrid cracker-cookie, and a watch; and set D was composed of two shoes, two socks, a hybrid shoe-sock, and a key. The hybrids and the typicals (a truck, a spoon, crackers, and a shoe) are shown in Figure 1. The drawing most dissimilar to the others in each set (the hand, the fish, the watch, or the key) was included to identify cases in which children selected randomly. It was assumed that, except for the hybrids, the names of all objects were familiar to children as young as 23 months old; this assumption is supported by the results of experiment 1 as well as the published norms. In addition, an actual spoon, fork, cracker, cookie, shoe, sock, toy car, and toy truck were used to test the 2-year-olds' knowledge of the pairs of familiar names before the trained name task was administered.

Procedure

Children were tested individually either in their homes or in a private room at their school or day-care center by a male and a female experimenter. Half of every age × sex subgroup were given the two tasks in one order and half in the opposite order; the entire procedure lasted from 30 to

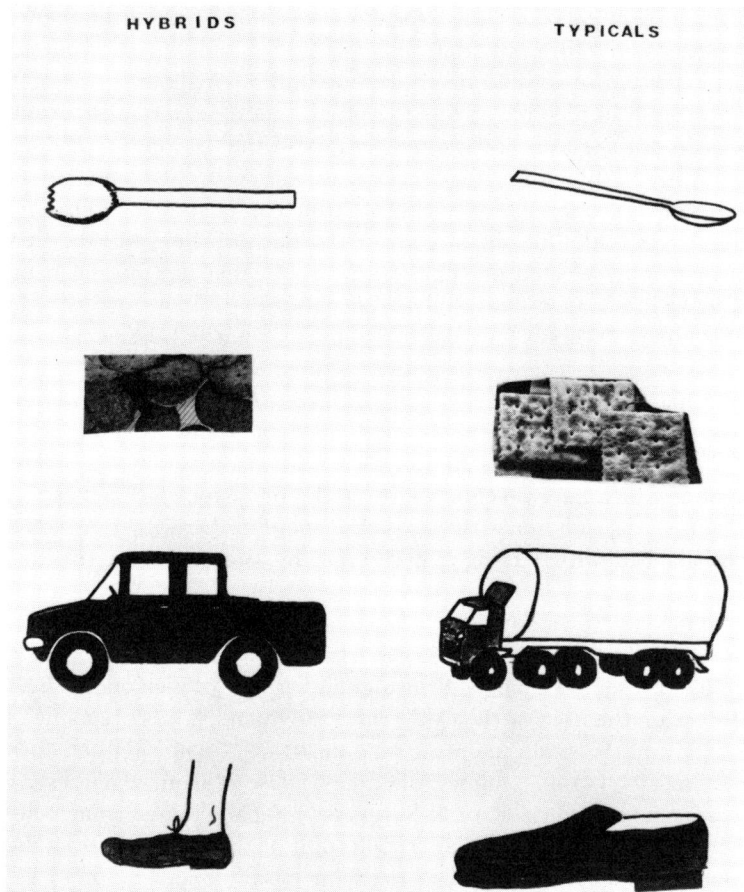

FIG. 1.—Referents of the trained name

45 min. All 2-year-olds were pretested for their comprehension of the familiar names used in the trained name task. This involved presenting eight objects (one referent of each of the names) and then asking the child to find the "*Y*" where *Y* was one of the familiar names; the names were tested in a random order.

Disambiguation test.—After establishing rapport, the female experimenter showed the child each drawing from set 1 or 2 (see Table 4) and asked him to name them; to minimize frustration, an old kind was always presented both before and after a new kind. The other experimenter recorded the child's responses. Whenever the child named a picture incorrectly, the female experimenter corrected him by saying, "No, that's not a [child's incorrect label]," but did not name the picture herself. If a child requested a picture's name, the experimenter either ignored the request or responded, "You'll find out later."

After the entire set had been presented, the female experimenter engaged the child in free play while the other experimenter constructed two sets of pairs for the test. For the first set, six of the drawings that the child could not name (by either a correct or an incorrect old name) were randomly selected; if necessary, drawings to which an old name had been overextended were added to obtain a set of six. Each of these was then paired with a randomly selected old kind from the set that had not been preexposed to yield six new kind–old token versus old kind–new token pairs similar to the N-O versus O-N pairs used in experiment 1. Drawing type was counterbalanced with left-right position. For the second set, old kinds that the child had named correctly during preexposure were randomly selected and paired with randomly selected old kinds from the set that had not been preexposed. The result was six old kind–old token versus old kind–new token pairs, which have no counterpart in the first experiment; these served as the control for whether subjects ignored requests. Drawing type was again counterbalanced with left-right position. The two sets were shuffled together.

The male experimenter told the child that there was another game to play. He then asked, "Do you know what an X is?" and, after the child responded, presented a pair of drawings and asked, "Which one is an X? Put your finger on the X." For the O-O versus O-N pairs, X was the name of the old token; for the other pairs, it was an artificial name (either "pilson," "repo," "hust," "syvane," "moog," or "tukey"). Use of artificial names made it unnecessary to include a set of N-N versus N-N pairs to determine whether the names were indeed unfamiliar. Selection of the new kind over the old was considered a correct response to the artificial name. The other experimenter recorded the child's responses.

On each trial, if the child selected an old kind–new token, the experimenter picked it up and asked, "What's another name for this?" If the child had not selected this object, the experimenter's question was, "What is this?" This procedure was used to ensure that what we defined as an old kind was indeed something the children could name.

Immediate correction and restriction tests.—An artificial name ("jegger" or "bave") was introduced for one of the drawings in two of the four sets (either the vehicles and food or the utensils and footwear). This drawing was a hybrid for half the children; for the rest, it was a typical referent (either a truck, a cracker, a spoon, or a shoe). The particular hybrid or typical named was counterbalanced. The male experimenter said to the child, "I am going to show you a jegger. Here is a jegger." He presented the drawing and said, "So this is a jegger. Isn't that neat? It's a jegger." The set of six pictures to which the named drawing belonged was then presented, and the child was asked, "Can you put your finger on a Y? Is there another Y?" If she said "yes," "Can you put your finger on it? Are there any more Y's?" If she said "yes," "Can you put your finger on them?" (Y was one of the two familiar basic-level names represented in the set.) The experimenter then repeated this questioning with the other familiar name. For example, a child might hear a truck called a jegger, then be asked whether any of the drawings of set A was a car and whether any was a truck. The set included the drawing the experimenter had called a jegger. When no artificial name was introduced, the children were still tested for their comprehension of the two familiar names represented in the set. Two orders of presentation of the four sets were used, with sets containing a named drawing occurring as often in each position as the other sets. The order of questioning about the two familiar names for a set was fixed; for example, "car" was always tested before "truck."

After all four sets had been presented, the experimenter showed the two sets that contained a named drawing. For each set, the child was asked to point to "the one I told you was a jegger/bave." This procedure was used to assess the child's retention of information about the referent of the trained name.

RESULTS

Disambiguation Test

The percentages of correct selections are shown in Table 5. A 3 (age) × 2 (kind of pair) mixed analysis of variance of the number of correct selections yielded significant effects of age, $F(2,45) = 25.42, p < .01$, kind of pair, $F(1,45) = 105.29, p < .01$, and age × kind of pair, $F(2,45) = 16.22, p < .01$. Correct selection of old kind–old tokens was nearly 100% in every age group. Newman-Keuls tests indicated that the 2-year-olds made significantly fewer correct selections of new kind–old tokens than either the 2½- or the 3½-year-olds, $p < .05$, but the latter two groups did not differ significantly from each other. Also, the 2-year-olds' selection of new kind–old tokens over old kind–new tokens was not significantly different from chance, but the older children's was.

When nearly all the new kinds were named by a child in the preexposure period, the set of new kind–old tokens was filled out with drawings she had named incorrectly. Although the experimenter corrected these overextensions, the child may not have accepted this correction. Only a fraction of the new kind trials consisted of these types of drawings—12%, 17%, and 21%, for the 2-, 2½-, and 3½-year-olds, respectively. If these trials as well as those in which the old kind–new token could not be named (13%, 11%, and

TABLE 5
Selections of the Correct Referent of a New Name

	Pair Type			
	New Kind–Old Token vs. Old Kind–New Token		Old Kind–Old Token vs. Old Kind–New Token	
Age	Raw Score	Adjusted Score	Raw Score	Adjusted Score
2-1	44	50	94	97
2-8	77	85	98	99
3-5	85	90	99	100

Note.—Entries are percentages based on six selections per subject, 16 subjects per age group. Adjusted scores are based only on trials in which the new kind was not called by an old name and the old kind was named correctly.

2%, respectively) are excluded, performance improves by only a few percentage points (see the corrected scores in Table 5), and the results of the analysis of variance are unchanged. The 2-year-olds were no better than chance at selecting new kinds over old as the referents of new names. In contrast to experiment 1, no age group exhibited a bimodal distribution of performance on new kinds versus old.

Immediate Correction Test

The 2-year-olds were pretested for their familiarity with the four pairs of "familiar" names used in the immediate correction test. The names were considered familiar if either the correct referent or the object from the same semantic field was selected. For example, when asked to "find the car," children could select either the car or the truck. Every 2-year-old knew every name, except for one who did not know "cracker."

The first analysis concerned children's tendencies to select either the hybrids or the typicals as referents of at least one of the two familiar names. There were a few test trials in which some refused to select drawings or selected the most dissimilar one (e.g., the hand as a referent of "car"). Considered as failures to comply with instruction, these instances constituted no more than 7% of the trials for any age group and were excluded from all analyses. The missing cells were filled by the mean score of the age group on the particular type of trial.

The percentage of trials in which hybrids and typicals were selected are summarized in Table 6. Entries marked with a superscript [a] are the percentages for pictures that served as referents of the trained names; the immediate correction effect is evident if these are lower than the other percentages for the same kind of drawing (hybrid or typical). This translates into the finding that three factors—whether a trained name was introduced

TABLE 6

SELECTIONS OF TYPICALS AND HYBRIDS AS REFERENTS OF AT LEAST ONE
OF TWO OLD NAMES IN EXPERIMENT 2

AGE AND REFERENT	SELECTIONS OF TYPICALS		SELECTIONS OF HYBRIDS	
	New Name Introduced	New Name Not Introduced	New Name Introduced	New Name Not Introduced
2-1:				
Typical	100[a]	94	84	87
Hybrid	100	100	67[a]	71
2-8:				
Typical	86[a]	100	100	94
Hybrid	100	100	47[a]	93
3-5:				
Typical	94[a]	100	100	88
Hybrid	100	100	56[a]	88

NOTE.—Entries are percentages based on two selections per subject, eight subjects per condition.
[a] These entries should be lower than the ones next to them in the row if immediate correction occurred.

for a picture set, whether it referred to a typical or a hybrid, and whether selections of hybrids or typicals are considered—interact in explaining the variance in picture selections.

A 3 (age) × 2 (drawing named: hybrid vs. typical) × 2 (whether new name introduced for a set) × 2 (drawing selected: hybrid vs. typical) mixed analysis of variance of the number of selections, in which the last two factors were within subjects, yielded significant effects of drawing named, $F(1,42) = 5.57, p < .05$, whether new name introduced, $F(1,42) = 8.84, p < .01$, and drawing selected, $F(1,42) = 22.62, p < .01$. More drawings were selected when two of the four typicals were named rather than two of the four hybrids. Consistent with the ME hypothesis, fewer drawings were selected when a new name had been introduced for one of the pictures in a set than when it had not. Also, more typicals than hybrids were selected. This last result validates our assumption that children were more certain that the typicals were referents of at least one of the familiar names than that the hybrids were. For example, the typical truck was selected as a referent of "truck" on nearly every trial, but the hybrid car-truck was not picked as a referent of either "truck" or "car" on 30% of the trials. Also, when selecting hybrids, children picked them first on only 20% of the trials, whereas they selected the typicals first in 44% of instances. The absence of a significant age × drawing selected interaction indicates that the assumption of differential certainty of typical versus hybrid membership is valid for all age groups.

Several interactions were significant: drawing named × whether new name introduced, $F(1,42) = 8.07, p < .01$; drawing named × drawing selected, $F(1,42) = 12.67, p < .01$; drawing named × whether new name introduced × drawing selected, $F(1,42) = 12.70$, $p < .01$; and the interaction of all four factors, $F(2,42) = 5.28$, $p < .01$. The most important effect is the four-way interaction because it indicates that the predicted three-way interaction was not obtained in every age group. Separate 2 (drawing named) × 2 (whether new name introduced) × 2 (drawing selected) mixed analyses of variance were conducted for each age group's selection data. A significant three-way interaction was obtained for 3½-year-olds, $F(1,14) = 7.23$, $p < .05$, and 2½-year-olds, $F(1,14) = 15.75$, $p < .01$, but not for 2-year-olds, $F(1,14) = .33$, $p > .1$. The 2-year-olds' selections were not affected by whether a name had been introduced for a drawing; the only significant effect indicates that they were more likely to select typicals than hybrids. The older children were less likely to select a hybrid drawing if the trained name had been introduced for it. Selection of typicals was not affected by introduction of the trained name in any age group. It should be noted, however, that the three cases in which a 2½- or a 3½-year-old failed to select a typical were all ones in which the trained name had been introduced for it.

Interpretation of the negative results for the 2-year-olds must be tempered by the results of the retention test for the trained name. These children had great difficulty identifying the drawings that had been used to train the new names. Only 40% of the hybrid condition's selections and 27% of the typical condition's selections were correct; given that there were six drawings to choose from, chance performance would be 17%. Thus, it may be that the 2-year-olds showed no immediate correction effect because they could not remember which drawing the experimenter had labeled with the new name. In three of the six instances in which a child in the hybrid condition passed the retention test for a new name, the hybrid was selected as a referent of a familiar name. In all four of such instances in the typical condition, the typical was selected as a referent of a familiar name. These cases are too infrequent, however, to make statistical comparisons to the respective base rates of 79% and 98%.

The retention of the older children was much better. In the hybrid condition, 93% of the 2½-year-olds' selections and 88% of the 3½-year-olds' selections were correct; in the typical condition, correct selections represented 50% and 69%, respectively. In 17 of the 19 instances in which a child in the typical condition passed the retention test, the typical was selected as a referent of a familiar name. Thus, memory failure is an unlikely explanation for why the older children's selection of typicals was unaffected by the introduction of new names or why their selection of hybrids was affected on only half the trials.

The ME bias does not strictly entail the immediate correction effect. Children can also either disambiguate or reject to preserve ME. Although we did not measure disambiguation, analysis of how children who showed no immediate correction effect reacted to the introduction of the new name suggests that they did not reject it. On only 6% of the trials did they offer any explicit resistance (e.g., saying, "No, it's a car," after the experimenter had called it a "bave"), and on 42% of the trials they actually imitated the name. Although they spontaneously produced the familiar name on 31% of the trials, they were not necessarily offering correction; in fact, on three trials (4%) they spontaneously combined the new with the familiar name (e.g., "jegger car").

Restriction Test

We analyzed instances in which children selected overlapping sets of drawings for the pairs of familiar names (e.g., at least one drawing was selected for both "sock" and "shoe"). The mean percentage of trials in which overlapping sets were selected was 50%, 38%, and 8% for the 2-, 2½-, and 3½-year-olds, respectively. A three-factor (age) one-way analysis of variance of these instances yielded a significant effect, $F(2,45) = 8.97$, $p < .01$. A Newman-Keuls test indicated that the 3½-year-olds were significantly less likely to allow overlaps than either group of younger children; the latter two did not differ significantly.

Subsequent analyses support the contention that these overlaps were not simply slips in performance. One could argue that they merely reflect indecision concerning the membership of the hybrid. However, in only 10% of the cases of overlap was the hybrid the only drawing selected for both names. Nor did indecision or memory failure concerning a single drawing produce the overlaps—69% of the cases involved more than one drawing.

In 42% of the instances of overlap, one name appeared to be subordinate to the other (e.g., two drawings were selected as both cars and trucks and two others as just cars). In 39%, neither name's extension was wholly within the other's (e.g., one drawing was selected as both a car and a truck, two others as just cars, and one other as just a truck); in 19%, the names appeared to be coextensive (e.g., three drawings were selected as both cars and trucks).

Relations between Tests

There were three measures of the ME bias in this experiment: the tendencies to pick the new kind in the disambiguation test, to avoid selecting the referent of a new name in the immediate correction test, and to keep the referents of two familiar names from overlapping in the restriction test. Although all these tendencies increased with age, there were no significant correlations among them (even when the data for hybrids and typicals were considered separately). However, the small number of test items on which these measures were based—six, four, and four, respectively—renders their reliability for individuals (as opposed to groups) suspect. Also, each measure is clearly affected by factors other than an ME bias. For example, a child who happened to extend a familiar name narrowly would be unlikely to allow it to overlap with other names even if she lacked an ME bias; similarly, a few of the children who were just guessing in the disambiguation test should have selected a high number of new kinds by chance. Such random factors attenuate correlations but have less effect on group comparisons where they tend to cancel one another. Even at the group level, however, the measures of the ME bias exhibited developmental asynchrony. For example, nearly every 2½-year-old chose new kinds over old in the disambiguation test, but only some kept the referents of familiar names from overlapping, and even fewer avoided assigning a familiar name to the training referent of a new name.

DISCUSSION

General Implications

The results indicate that Merriman's (1986b) hypothesis that children under age 3 years have no ME bias needs revision. Although they did not show the restriction effect, 32-month-olds did produce both the disambiguation and the immediate correction effects. It is difficult to explain these findings without granting some kind of ME bias. However, it is also difficult to explain why this group did not also show the restriction effect. Recall that neither the disambiguation nor the correction effect is strictly entailed by the bias but that the restriction effect is. One possible explanation is that our test of restriction was insensitive because it did not include a control condition in which only one noun from each of the pairs of familiar names was tested. It may be that names would be generalized more broadly in this condition than when they are tested in pairs. For example, children might generalize "truck" more broadly if they had not just been asked to generalize "car" to the same set of pictures, even though they would allow "truck" and "car" to name some of the same pictures.

The simplest way to revise Merriman's hypothesis is to lower his estimate of the age at which the bias emerges to somewhere between 25 and 32 months of age. Unlike the older children, 25-month-olds showed no tendency to disambiguate, immediately correct, or restrict. Their failure to disambiguate suggests that they lack not only an ME bias but also a bias to fill lexical gaps (i.e., to find new names for new kinds), contrary to Clark's (1987) claim.

Since they performed poorly in the test of new name retention, the 25-month-olds' failure to show the immediate correction effect should be interpreted with caution. However, given their failure to disambiguate, it is unlikely they would be capable of showing this effect. The immediate correction effect requires that the ME bias be strong enough to override belief in the correctness of an old name, doubt in an adult's authority as a namer, and difficulty in isolating distinctive object properties. In contrast, the disambiguation effect requires only the weakest of biases. It is also possible that the retention test overestimated the number of children who could not remember the referent of the trained name at the time they were selecting referents of the familiar names. The questions about the latter were posed immediately after the new name was trained, but the retention test was administered after all eight familiar names had been tested. Thus, some children may have retained information about the trained name long enough for it potentially to influence their decisions about the familiar names but not long enough to pass the retention test. The former requires only that the information still be in short-term memory, whereas the latter requires that it be in long-term memory and that retroactive interference not block access to it.

The Improved Test of Disambiguation

The criticisms of the disambiguation test used in experiment 1—that the toddlers may have disregarded instructions or believed the new kinds to be old kinds—cannot be applied to the version used in the present experiment. The 25-month-olds' willingness to follow instructions was evident in their near-perfect performance on the old name trials that were interspersed with the new name trials, and the pretest eliminated any new kinds that the children believed to be old kinds.

The procedural revisions may have been responsible for improvements in the children's performance. Unlike in experiment 1, 25-month-olds' performance on new kind–old token versus old kind–new token pairs was not below chance level, and the 32-month-olds performed better than the 36-month-olds of the first experiment. However, the revisions responsible for this improvement cannot be identified without further study. The present experiment involved much briefer preexposure than experiment 1, and this could have been less effective in reducing the novelty of the new kinds, thereby improving the performance of children who chose on the basis of novelty. Thus, although we can conclude that the majority of children do not show a disambiguation effect for new kind–old tokens until after age 25 months, we cannot identify the precise age at which they begin to show the effect.

MONOGRAPHS

The Effect of Typicality on Immediate Correction

The results of the present experiment indicated that children are more likely to correct an atypical than a typical referent of a familiar name following the introduction of a new name. When told that a typical looking shoe was a "jegger," for example, children showed no tendency to make "jegger" mutually exclusive with "shoe." However, when told that something that looked like a cross between a shoe and a sock was a "jegger," about half of both the 2½- and the 3½-year-olds made the name mutually exclusive with both "shoe" and "sock." The children who did not hear this object called a "jegger" showed very little tendency to restrict it from the extensions of the familiar names. Both this result and Merriman's (1986b) finding that variations in input can affect immediate correction support the claim that young preschoolers' ME bias acts as a kind of default option, that is, that they impose ME only if other sources of information do not strongly contradict it.

The finding of a typicality effect also converges with Anglin's (1977) finding that preschoolers were less likely to accept superordinate names for familiar than for unfamiliar objects only when the objects were atypical. In the light of the many differences between the two studies, the convergence is compelling.

The finding of a typicality effect in children as young as 32 months has implications for a current debate over the causes of children's underextensions of basic-level nouns. Both Adams and Bullock (1986) and Whitehurst, Kedesdy, and White (1982) have observed that mothers are much more likely to introduce new subordinate names for atypical than for typical referents of the basic-level nouns their children know; for example, they will tell their children that a chihuahua is a "chihuahua" but that a cocker spaniel is a "dog." Whitehurst et al. have argued that this pattern of input is primarily responsible for children's tendency to underextend basic-level names by excluding atypicals. However, Mervis and Rosch (1981) have argued that it is the lower family resemblance of atypicals that accounts for this tendency, and their argument is supported by evidence from training studies in which names are introduced for typicals and atypicals equally frequently (e.g., Rosch, Simpson, & Miller, 1976). Our findings indicate that family resemblance, input, and child age interact to account for children's underextension of basic-level names. For the two oldest groups in our experiment, variations in input only affected the assignment of atypicals (objects with lower family resemblance): when no name was introduced, these were selected as referents of familiar names as frequently as typicals; when a new name was introduced, they were selected less frequently. For the youngest children, name introduction had no effect; the atypicals were always selected less frequently than the typicals.

Our results concerning immediate correction are somewhat discrepant with those Merriman (1986b) obtained: the 2½-year-olds in our hybrid condition showed a significant tendency to immediately correct, whereas the 2½-year-olds in Merriman's study did not. In the latter, two new names were trained for a set of artificial objects, and the second name was introduced for an object the children had just selected as a referent of the first. In the present experiment, children in the hybrid condition learned a new name for an atypical referent of a familiar real name. The difference between these two tasks that may be responsible for the discrepant results can be determined only through further experimentation. Merriman's subjects may have been less willing to immediately correct because the old name had been learned only 10 min earlier from a single example, or because immediate correction entailed a public admission of error, or because the new name had been introduced for an object that too closely resembled the training referent of the old name (with consequences similar to those for the typical referent in the present experiment).

Relations between Tests

Our hypothesis that the immediate correction and restriction effects are weaker than the disambiguation effect was confirmed. The 2½- and the 3½-year-olds gave correct answers on nearly every trial of the disambiguation test but immediately corrected on no trials in the typicals condition and half the trials in the hybrid condition. Many 2½-year-olds failed to show the restriction effect for some pairs of familiar basic-level names. The immediate correction and restriction effects will occur only if the ME bias is strong enough to "defeat" other biases and beliefs, whereas the disambiguation effect will occur even if the bias is weak. The latter effect can occur even without the bias if children have a bias to fill lexical gaps (i.e., to avoid letting new kinds go without names). If children believed that new names should refer to new kinds rather than old but did not believe that names should be mutually exclusive, they would not be violating the laws of logic. Although the latter belief logically entails the former, the converse is not true.

V. EXPERIMENT 3: IMMEDIATE CORRECTION AND RESTRICTION BY CHILDREN AND ADULTS— LINGUISTIC AND METALINGUISTIC MEASURES

Two-Year-Olds

Although 24-month-olds showed no signs of having an ME bias in either experiment 1 or experiment 2, some problems with the tests of immediate correction and restriction in the second experiment weaken the case against this age group. First, there was some evidence that instruction concerning the new name might not have been remembered, and this could account for the toddlers' failure to immediately correct. Steps were taken in experiment 3 to improve the effectiveness of name training and hence improve memory for the name's referent. Second, although they failed to show the restriction effect on 50% of test trials, it is still possible that 24-month-olds have a weak restriction tendency that does not entirely prevent overlaps of extension but does limit them. This possibility can be assessed by examining whether generalization of a familiar name becomes narrower after a related name has been generalized to the same set of test objects. For example, will children identify fewer objects as referents of "truck" if they have just identified some of them as referents of "car"? This could not be assessed in experiment 2 because pairs of familiar names were tested in a fixed order (e.g., "car" was always tested before "truck"); in the present experiment, order was counterbalanced.

After Early Childhood

Experiments 1 and 2, together with Merriman's (1986b) study, support the claim that the ME bias grows stronger during early childhood. Little is known about the fate of the bias after early childhood, however. In the only relevant study, Markman et al. (1980) found that children as old as 14 years tended to deny that a trained superordinate noun could be used to name individual objects. Although an ME bias could account for this error, there are alternative explanations; for instance, it could be due to the difficulty of abstracting superordinate classes. On the other hand, although 17-year-olds avoided this error, they may still have a default-option ME bias; they may have realized that the syntactic information in the training sentences (e.g., "These are ——s") indicated that the names designated two overlapping classes and that input cues thus contradicted an ME interpretation. To gather more information about the nature of the bias beyond the preschool years, 2-, 6-, 11-, and 19-year-olds were given tests of both immediate correction and restriction.

Although there have been no assessments of the bias in adults, the results of an experiment by Glucksberg and Danks (1968) on adults' functional fixedness are suggestive of its presence. Only 5% of a group of adults could solve a problem that required them to use a screwdriver in an unconventional way—as a conductor of electricity. However, when instructed to call the screwdriver by a nonsense label, 31% solved the conduction problem. A second experiment in which subjects were told to use no label suggested that the release from functional fixedness (thinking only about an object's conventional functions) was caused by using the new name rather than by not using the old one. One explanation for these findings is that, because adults believe a new name means something different than a familiar one, they tend to think about properties that are not part of the latter's meaning, including unconventional object functions, when interpreting the former. Thus, those instructed to call the screwdriver a "bream" tended to think about properties other than the ones important for calling it a "screwdriver" and hence were more likely to think about its function as a conductor. These results suggest the presence of the kind of contrastive bias proposed by Clark (1987), if not of the ME bias.

Adults should have a default-option ME bias. For any word, the number of other words that share its referents is an infinitesimal fraction of the total number included in the dictionary; if one has no information about a new word, it is safe to bet that it does not share referents with any particular familiar word. Such a disposition may underlie adults' impression, first described by Brown (1958), that, although there are often many acceptable names for something, one name seems to "fit" the thing much better than all the others. Although Rosch, Mervis, et al. (1976) have shown that this best-fitting or basic-level name tends to map to a category with certain optimal properties, these properties seem insufficient to create the impression that there is only one true name for anything. Alternatively, the primacy of the basic level in adults' thinking about names may be the source of the impression because, at that basic level, there is only one name for anything. Finally, the common question, "What is this called?" seems to presuppose the existence of one and only one name for the referent in question.

MONOGRAPHS

Metalinguistic Status of the Bias

There has been no research on the metalinguistic status of the bias. The present experiment assessed the extent to which the bias is manifest both in definitions of new names for old names' referents and in responses to direct questions about whether such names are subordinate to the old names. The two metalinguistic measures were analyzed for their interrelation as well as for their relation to a linguistic measure of the bias—the immediate correction effect.

There is a small but rapidly growing body of research concerning the development of word definition. This topic is worthy of study because the ability to reflect on and articulate the meaning of words undoubtedly contributes to success in reading and writing (Just & Carpenter, 1987; Nystrand, 1982). Moreover, tests of word reference can never fully reveal children's understanding of word meaning because, as Anglin (1985) has pointed out, such tests have numerous methodological inadequacies, some words have no reference (e.g., "idea," "why"), and an indefinite number of definitions can be constructed for any extension. (Anglin credits this last point to Goodman, 1972.) To appreciate the last point, consider that two physical properties may be perfectly correlated (e.g., having three sides and having angles that sum to 180°), yet a child might consider only one to be important to the meaning of the name for things with these properties (e.g., "triangle"), and hence the second property could not be identified by tests in which the child is asked to select the word's referents. Thus, children's definitions may provide some new information about what words mean to them.

With age, children's definitions of concrete nouns become increasingly structured both syntactically and semantically (Litowitz, 1977; Watson, 1985). Watson (1985) has described the following rules that constrain the construction of such definitions, in order of increasing restrictiveness:

a) a syntactically acceptable predicate of the definiendum (e.g., saying, "It barks," or, "It has a tail");
b) a syntactically acceptable predicate of the definiendum that begins with the copula "is" (e.g., saying, "It is furry");
c) "is" plus a noun phrase (e.g., saying, "It is something that likes to be petted");
d) "is" plus a noun phrase headed by a class name (e.g., "It is an animal that barks and has a tail").

Definitions tend to become more accurate, detailed, and consensual (one child's tends to match another's) as children grow older (Anglin, 1985;

Norlin, 1981; Schmidt & Shatz, 1986; Wehren, DeLisi, & Arnold, 1981). The extent to which choices on tests of word reference fit the criteria mentioned in definitions also tends to increase (Anglin, 1977). However, even older children show great inconsistency from word to word in both the structure and the content of definitions (Anglin, 1985).

Both Anglin (1977) and Karmiloff-Smith (1986) have documented that children may adhere to complex rules in word use before they articulate them in metalinguistic tasks; there may even be a lag between the point at which children are guided by a rule and the point at which they become aware of it. Thus, although 6-year-olds are compelled by an ME bias to show disambiguation, immediate correction, or restriction effects in tests of word use, they may be neither aware of this bias nor able to describe it. Experiment 1 already provided evidence of one kind of lag between linguistic and metalinguistic measures of lexical knowledge—many children interpreted a new name as referring to a new kind rather than an old, indicating that they had identified the name as being new yet claimed familiarity with it.

The present experiment differs from previous research on noun definition in that older children and adults did not have the advantage of having known the definienda longer than the younger children; the learning experience was controlled. Second, subjects knew very little about the definienda; they had seen only a drawing of a single referent. Finally, the definienda were clearly related to familiar basic-level names. Thus, the definitions provided under these conditions should shed some light on the generality and causes of the developmental trends noted in previous research. For example, the trends toward increasing consensus and mention of class names may depend heavily on experience with the definienda; if so, these should not be obtained in the present experiment.

METHOD

Subjects

Four groups of 24 subjects, aged, respectively, 2 years ($M = 2$-0, range = 1-10–2-4), 6 years ($M = 6$-2, range = 5-2–6-10), 11 years ($M = 11$-1, range = 10-7–11-8), and 19 years ($M = 19$-9, range = 18-4–21-6), participated. Six 2-year-olds were replaced because they stopped cooperating during the procedure. The 2-year-olds were located through published birth records, the 6- and 11-year-olds were students from local elementary schools, and the adults were students in an introductory psychology course who received credit for their participation. Each age group was predominantly middle class and contained as many males as females.

MONOGRAPHS

Materials

The 24 drawings from the trained name task of experiment 2 were used.

Procedure

Each participant was tested individually by a female experimenter: the 2-year-olds in their homes; the 6- and 11-year-olds in a private room at their schools; and the adults in a lab room at the university.

The procedure was the same as in the trained name task of experiment 2, with the following exceptions. The 2-year-olds were not pretested for knowledge of the familiar names because the pretesting of the second experiment indicated that these names were quite familiar to this age group. An artificial name ("bave," "danker," "hust," and "pilson") was trained for a drawing of each set rather than just two of the sets. For half the subjects, the drawing was a hybrid; for the rest, it was a typical. Training consisted of extensive repetition of a name as well as several attempts to elicit imitation of it. The order in which familiar names were tested was counterbalanced with age and sex. After the last familiar name was tested, each set of six drawings was presented again, and retention of the trained name was tested. After the test, a set was removed, and the subject was then asked, "What is an X? Is an X a kind of Y? Is an X a kind of Z?" where X was the trained name and Y and Z were the two familiar names. For example, the subject might be asked, "What is a bave? Is a bave a kind of spoon? Is a bave a kind of fork?" The 2-year-olds were not asked these follow-up questions because pilot testing, as well as previous research (Anglin, 1985), indicated that they would not comprehend them.

RESULTS

Immediate Correction Test

The 2-year-olds failed to comply with instructions on 12% of the familiar name test trials. These trials were excluded from all analyses, and the missing cells were filled by mean scores.

The percentage of trials in which hybrids and typicals were selected are summarized in Table 7; italicized entries are the percentages for trials in which the new name was trained for these drawings. The immediate correction effect is evident if these percentages are lower than those for trials in which the new name was trained for some other drawing (i.e., if the entry marked with the superscript a is lower than the figure either above or below

TABLE 7

SELECTIONS OF TYPICALS AND HYBRIDS AS
REFERENTS OF AT LEAST ONE OF TWO
OLD NAMES IN EXPERIMENT 3

AGE AND REFERENT	DRAWINGS SELECTED	
	Typicals	Hybrids
2:		
Typical	98[a]	92
Hybrid	93	84[a]
6:		
Typical	90[a]	94
Hybrid	100	42[a]
11:		
Typical	100[a]	92
Hybrid	100	73[a]
19:		
Typical	94[a]	94
Hybrid	100	50[a]

NOTE.—Entries are percentages based on four selections per subject, 12 subjects per condition.
[a] These entries should be lower than the ones directly above or below them if immediate correction occurred.

it in Table 7). A 4 (age) × 2 (drawing named: hybrid vs. typical) × 2 (drawing selected: hybrid vs. typical) mixed analysis of variance of the number of selections, in which the last factor was within subjects, yielded significant effects of age, $F(3,88) = 3.00, p < .05$, drawing named, $F(1,88) = 22.06, p < .01$, drawing selected, $F(1,88) = 48.32, p < .01$, age × drawing selected, $F(3,88) = 2.85, p < .05$, drawing named × drawing selected, $F(1,88) = 35.53, p < .01$, and age × drawing named × drawing selected, $F(3,88) = 5.83, p < .01$.

As in experiment 2, typicals were nearly always selected as referents of a familiar name, but hybrids were selected on only 80% of the trials. This result validates the assumption that subjects were more certain that a familiar name applied to a typical than to a hybrid.

A familiar name was less likely to be accepted for drawings that had been designated by a new name; however, this result was true only of some age groups' judgments of hybrid drawings. As in experiment 2, the 2-year-olds' judgments were not affected, $t(22) = 1.31, p > .10$. The 11-year-olds' judgments were also not affected, $t(22) = 1.53, p = .07$, but those of the 6- and 19-year-olds were, $t(22) > 3.14, p < .01$. Follow-up analyses indicated that the effect of hearing a new name for a hybrid was significantly greater for the 6- and 19-year-olds than for the 2-year-olds, $p < .05$. All other paired comparisons were not significant, although the 6- versus 11-year-old comparison was marginal, $t(22) = 2.00, p < .06$.

MONOGRAPHS

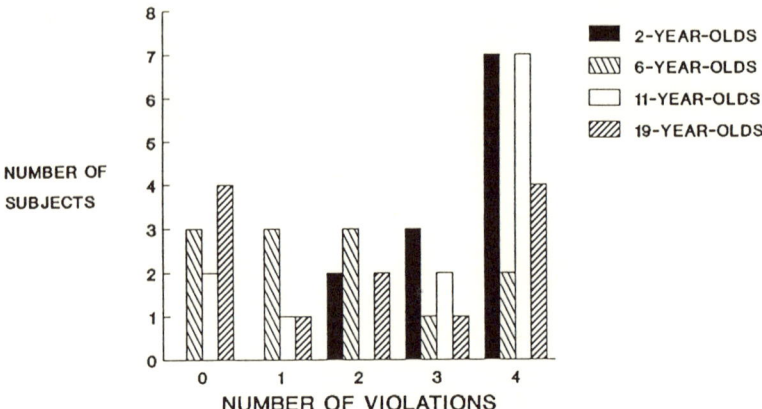

FIG. 2.—Distribution of frequencies of ME violation by subjects in the hybrid condition

The distribution of frequencies with which individuals violated ME by applying a familiar name to a previously named hybrid are presented in Figure 2. The 11-year-olds' distribution was more similar to that of the 19- than the 2-year-olds. Three 11- and four 19-year-olds showed consistent immediate correction, but none of the 2-year-olds did. The two oldest groups tended either to avoid the hybrid consistently or to select it consistently; the 6-year-olds were less consistent; and the 2-year-olds either consistently selected the hybrid or were inconsistent.

As in experiment 2, the 2-year-olds had difficulty remembering which drawing had been the training referent of the new name. Those in the hybrid and typical conditions selected correctly on only 45% and 19% of the retention trials, respectively. However, in 15 of the 19 cases in which they remembered that the hybrid had been the training referent, they also accepted one of the familiar names for it. Thus, memory failure is an unlikely explanation for why introduction of a new name had no effect on their acceptance of familiar names for hybrids. The older subjects' memory was quite good; they selected correctly on 99% of the hybrid and 92% of the typical retention trials. Thus, memory failure is an unlikely explanation for why their acceptance of familiar names for typicals was not affected by the introduction of a new name or why their acceptance for hybrids was affected on only a fraction of the trials.

Restriction Test

As in experiment 2, only the 2-year-olds showed a substantial tendency to allow the pairs of familiar names to share referents. The percentage of trials in which overlapping sets were selected was 51%, 3%, 4%, and 5% for the 2-, 6-, 11-, and 19-year-olds, respectively. A four-factor (age) one-way analysis of variance and follow-up Newman-Keuls comparisons confirmed that 2-year-olds chose overlapping sets more often than the older age groups. The latter groups even refrained from assigning the ambiguous hybrids to more than one name. The 2-year-olds' tendency to violate ME could not be attributed to mere indecision concerning a single drawing such as the hybrid: only 12% of the cases of overlap involved solely the hybrid, and only 40% involved only a single drawing. When the 2-year-olds' selections overlapped, they were more likely to treat one name as subordinate to another (42% of the cases) or to include neither name's extension wholly within the other's (49%) than to treat the names as having exactly the same extension (9%).

The 2-year-olds also failed to show a "weak" restriction effect; the number of referents they selected was unaffected by whether a familiar name was tested before or after its contrastive name, $t(23) = .82$, $p > .10$. An average of 2.90 and 2.76 pictures were selected on first and second tests, respectively. Also, given the average for first tests, no more than 2.10 should have been selected on second tests because test sets contained only five potential referents (e.g., two cars, two trucks, and a car-truck were the only potential referents of "car" and "truck"); in fact, the average for second tests was significantly greater than this figure, $t(23) = 4.02$, $p < .01$.

Definitions of the Trained Names

Definitions of the trained names were classified according to the following scheme:

1. INCLUSION.—The definiendum was either equated or subordinated to some other name(s), implying that its extension was included in that of the other name(s). The four subtypes differed only in terms of the names given:

a) *Both the familiar names* (= FN & FN):

e.g., "A bave is a $\begin{bmatrix} \text{truck and a car} \\ \text{half car and half truck} \\ \text{cross between a car and a truck} \\ \text{car-truck} \end{bmatrix}$."

b) *One of the familiar names* (= FN):

e.g., "A bave $\begin{bmatrix} \text{is a} \\ \text{is a kind of} \\ \text{is a sort of} \\ \text{is a type of} \\ \text{might be a} \end{bmatrix} \begin{bmatrix} \text{truck} \\ \text{semi} \end{bmatrix}$."

c) *Some other familiar name* (= ON):

e.g., Same as the example for 1b except substitute "tractor" for "truck/semi."

d) *A superordinate name* (= SUPO):

e.g., Same as the example for 1b except substitute "vehicle" for "truck/semi." This category did not include responses that identified the definiendum as "something," "thing," or "object" or that also mentioned a more specific name.

2. COMPARISON.—The definiendum was compared to another name. Responses that equated or subordinated it to one name and compared it to another were classified as inclusions. Subtype again depended on the name given:

a) *One of the familiar names* (like FN):

e.g., "A bave
$\begin{bmatrix} \text{is like a} \\ \text{looks like a} \\ \text{is kind of like a} \\ \text{is kind of a} \\ \text{is sorta like a} \\ \text{kinda looks like a} \\ \text{is like a kind of} \end{bmatrix}$
$\begin{bmatrix} \text{truck} \\ \text{semi} \end{bmatrix}$."

b) *Some other familiar name* (like ON):

e.g., Same as the example for 2a except substitute "tractor" for "truck/semi."

3. PART.—The definiendum was identified as a part (e.g., "A bave is the front part of a car").

4. DESCRIBE.—Physical or functional properties were described (e.g., "A bave has got four wheels and four side windows and it's red"). A response was assigned to this category only if it did not fit one of the others; for instance, "A bave is a truck with four doors" was categorized as FN.

5. NO ANSWER.

Each definition was assigned to a single category by the first author. A second rater scored 25% of the transcripts; the interrater reliability—(number of agreements)/(number of agreements + disagreements)—was .96.

The results are summarized in Table 8. A 3 (age) × 2 (drawing named: typical vs. hybrid) multivariate analysis of variance of the frequency of each definition subtype yielded a significant effect of drawing named, $F(8,59) = 13.2$, $p < .01$. The same sensitivity to object typicality was evident in

TABLE 8

TYPES OF DEFINITIONS GIVEN FOR THE TRAINED NAMES

REFERENT AND AGE	Inclusion				Comparison					
	= FN & FN	= FN	= ON	= SUPO	Like FN	Like ON	Part	Describe	No Answer
Typical:									
6	0	98	0	0	0	0	0	2	0
11	0	79	0	0	0	0	15	0	2
19	0	88	2	0	6	0	0	4	0
Hybrid:									
6	8	50	10	0	15	4	0	11	2
11	19	29	0	6	37	4	4	0	0
19	25	46	2	6	17	0	2	2	0

NOTE.—Entries are percentages based on four definitions per subject, 12 subjects per condition.

TABLE 9

Definitions of the Trained Names That Satisfied Constraints on Form and Content

	Constraints				
Referent and Age	Predicate	"Is" + Predicate	"Is" + Noun Phrase	Class Name	Aristotelian Definition
Typical:					
6	100	100	100	98	17
	(100)	(100)	(100)	(100)	(17)
11	100	94	94	79	8
	(98)	(98)	(98)	(83)	(15)
19	100	98	98	90	29
	(100)	(100)	(100)	(94)	(29)
Hybrid:					
6	98	89	73	69	15
	(96)	(89)	(85)	(23)	
11	98	96	56	54	33
	(98)	(98)	(94)	(69)	
19	100	81	79	77	48
	(100)	(100)	(98)	(58)	

Note.—Entries are percentages based on four definitions per subject, 12 subjects per condition. Entries in parentheses are percentages that satisfy the constraints if either "looks like" or "is like" is permitted to substitute for "is."

definitions as in referent selections. When the trained name was introduced for a typical rather than a hybrid referent, subjects were more likely to identify it with the referent's familiar name, $F(1,66) = 73.2, p < .01$, or with some other familiar name, $F(1,66) = 23.3, p < .01$, and were less likely to identify it with two familiar names, $F(1,66) = 19.2, p < .01$, to identify it with a superordinate, $F(1,66) = 6.49, p < .05$, or to compare it to a familiar name, $F(1,66) = 17.4, p < .01$.

Neither the age effect, $F(16,118) = 1.62, p = .08$, nor the age × drawing named interaction, $F(16,118) = 1.60, p = .08$, obtained significance, although both were marginal. Thus, each age group showed the same pattern of definitions.

The percentages that fit Watson's (1985) constraints are listed in the first four columns of Table 9. The fifth column contains the percentages that satisfied an additional restriction on her last constraint—not only did the definitions have to have an "is" + class name form, but the class name also had to be modified (e.g., "A bave is a *big* truck," or, "A pilson is a cracker *with seeds on it*"). Classic Aristotelian or scientific definitions take this form (Litowitz, 1977; Watson, 1985). The percentages decline as the table is read from left to right because all definitions that satisfy a particular constraint necessarily satisfy all constraints listed to the left of it (e.g., any response of the form "is" + NP is also a syntactically acceptable predicate beginning with "is"). The percentages listed in parentheses in the table are for definitions that fit somewhat looser versions of Watson's constraints—ones in which "looks like" and "is like" are allowed to substitute for "is." All definitions that were comparisons rather than inclusions could satisfy only these modified constraints.

The results contrast with those obtained by Watson (1985) and others (Anglin, 1977; Norlin, 1981) for familiar concrete nouns. In Watson's study, only 6% of 5-year-olds' and 44% of 10-year-olds' responses satisfied the "is" + class name constraint. In the present study, 66%–83% of the definitions of each age group fit this rule, and an even greater percentage fit the "is/is like/looks like" + class name rule. A 3 (age) × 2 (drawing named: typical vs. hybrid) analysis of variance of the number of definitions that satisfied the "is" + class name constraint yielded only a significant effect of drawing named, $F(1,66) = 17.34$, $p < .01$. More of the definitions of typicals than of hybrids had this format; however, this effect is not significant if "is like" and "looks like" are accepted as substitutes for "is," $F(1,66) = .03$.

The only constraint that varied with respect to age and drawing named was the most restrictive one, the Aristotelian form. Definitions of this type were given more frequently by the older groups, $F(2,66) = 4.00$, $p < .05$, and by the groups who heard the trained names applied to the hybrids rather than the typicals, $F(1,66) = 4.89$, $p < .05$. These effects were significant even when "is like" and "looks like" were accepted as substitutes for "is."

Answers to Subordination Questions

After defining the trained name, subjects were asked whether it was subordinate to either of the familiar names (e.g., "Is a bave a kind of car? Is a bave a kind of truck?"). Three patterns of response were possible—"no" to both questions, indicating that it is mutually exclusive with both names; "no" to one question and "yes" to the other, indicating that it is mutually exclusive with one but subordinate to the other; and "yes" to both questions, indicating that it is subordinate to both. The percentages of responses that fit each pattern (which we label "mutually exclusive," "single subordinate," and "double subordinate," respectively) are presented in the rightmost column of Table 10, under the heading "Subordination." A 3 (age) × 2 (drawing named: typical vs. hybrid) multivariate analysis of variance of the frequency of these response patterns yielded only a significant effect of drawing named, $F(2,65) = 28.12$, $p < .01$. Those who heard the name for a typical rather than a hybrid were more likely to give a single subordinate interpretation, $F(1,66) = 56.77$, $p < .01$, and less likely to interpret the name as a double subordinate, $F(1,66) = 35.77$, $p < .01$. Although the trend was only marginal, those in the typicals condition were also less likely to say "no" to both subordination questions, $F(1,66) = 3.44$, $p = .07$. Thus, responses to subordination questions were sensitive to typicality but not in the same way as definitions or referent selections (which were used to index the immediate correction effect).

Relations among Measures

A subject who must decide how the extension of a new name relates to those of two familiar names has several options. Three of these are ME (e.g., that a bave is neither a car nor a truck), single subordination (e.g., that a bave is either a car or a truck), and double subordination (e.g., that a bave is both a car and a truck). In the present experiment, there were three ways to estimate preferences for each type of interpretation: from selections of referents of the familiar names; from definitions of the trained name; and from answers to subordination questions. The first type of response is linguistic, whereas the last two are metalinguistic (because language is the object of judgment). The decision about which of the three interpretations is implied by a particular response is straightforward, with the exception of definitions. For these, the = FN & FN response was considered to imply double subordination, the = FN response to imply single subordination, and any other response to imply ME. This method may overestimate the frequency of ME interpretations and underestimate that of the other types because responses such as = SUPO or DESCRIBE do not strictly entail ME. For example, a subject who says, "A hust is an eating utensil," or, "A hust has a scoop on the end with points," may believe that a hust is a spoon, or a fork, or both. On the other hand, the modal definition identified the trained name by at least one of the familiar names, suggesting that this is the first kind of definition subjects consider giving and that other kinds are offered only if this kind is thought to be incorrect. Because the issue cannot be resolved, the frequency estimates derived from the definitions must be interpreted cautiously. Table 10 presents estimates, derived from the different measures, of the relative frequency of the three interpretations.

Although each measure was sensitive to object typicality and insensitive to age (over the range from 6 to 19 years), each was differentially sensitive to typicality. The locus of this differential sensitivity was the hybrid condition. Separate 3 (age) × 2 (drawing named: typical vs. hybrid) × 3 (measure) mixed analyses of variance, in which the last factor was within subjects, of the frequency of each type of interpretation supported these conclusions. The analyses revealed significant effects of drawing named on each type of interpretation, $F(1,66) > 30.2$, $p < .01$, of measure on ME and double subordinate interpretations, $F(2,132) > 15.4$, $p < .01$, but, most important,

TABLE 10

THREE MEASURES OF THE RELATION OF THE TRAINED NAME TO THE
TWO FAMILIAR ONES

	MEASURE		
REFERENT, AGE, AND RELATION	Referent Selection	Definition	Subordination
Typical:			
6:			
Mutually exclusive	10	2	2
Single subordinate	90	98	96
Double subordinate	0	0	0
11:			
Mutually exclusive	0	21	6
Single subordinate	100	79	92
Double subordinate	0	0	2
19:			
Mutually exclusive	6	12	2
Single subordinate	94	88	94
Double subordinate	0	0	4
Hybrid:			
6:			
Mutually exclusive	58	42	15
Single subordinate	40	50	56
Double subordinate	2	8	29
11:			
Mutually exclusive	27	52	10
Single subordinate	65	29	40
Double subordinate	8	19	50
19:			
Mutually exclusive	50	29	4
Single subordinate	50	46	63
Double subordinate	0	25	33

NOTE.—Entries are percentages based on four responses per subject, 12 subjects per condition.

of drawing named × measure on ME and double subordinate interpretations, $F(2,132) > 9.4, p < .01$. Irrespective of measure, subjects in the typical condition showed a strong tendency to supply single subordinate interpretations; they gave this interpretation on an average of 93% of the trials. Separate 3 (age) × 3 (measure) mixed analyses of variance of the frequency with which they gave each type of interpretation yielded no significant effects. On the other hand, a similar analysis of the hybrid condition yielded a significant effect of measure on both ME interpretations, $F(2,66) = 16.44, p < .01$, and double subordinate interpretations, $F(2,66) = 26.91, p < .01$. The subordinate questions measure revealed a much higher tendency to allow overlapping extension—fewer ME interpretations (10% vs. 43%) and more double subordinate interpretations (37% vs. 11%)—than the other two measures. In addition, the definitions measure revealed a higher tendency toward double subordination than the referent selection measure (18% vs. 3%).

The responses of the subjects in the hybrid condition were further analyzed for within-subject consistency. Measures of the same interpretation (e.g., the referent selection and definition measures of ME) should be positively correlated, and measures of different interpretations (e.g., the referent selection measure of ME and the definition measure of single subordination) should be negatively correlated. If not, then either the interpretation that guides a subject's responses to the three measures is unstable or some of the measures are invalid (i.e., they do not measure the interpretations that we claim they do).

The intercorrelations presented in Table 11 show only modest within-subject consistency. All nine pairs of measures of the same interpretation were positively correlated (see n. a to the table). All but one of the 18 pairs of measures of different interpretations were negatively correlated. This pattern is significantly different from what would be expected by chance, $\Phi(N = 27$ pairs$) = .92$, $p < .01$. However, many correlations were not significantly different from zero. The average correlation between measures of the same interpretation was .30 and between measures of different interpretations $-.15$. (The intercorrelations between common measures of different interpretations are not reported in Table 11 because these estimates are not independent.)

DISCUSSION

Two-Year-Olds

Just as in the first two experiments, there were no signs of an ME bias among the 24-month-olds; they showed neither an immediate correction nor a restriction effect. Even discounting the performance of those who failed the retention test for the trained name, the remaining subgroup also showed no tendency to immediately correct. The failure to produce the restriction effect is remarkable because the test of this effect was more sensitive than that reported in experiment 2. If the children had had any tendency to avoid generalizing a name to a picture that they had just identified by another name, they should have generalized the second names tested less broadly than the first ones. They did not. Also, as in experiment 2, they were just as likely to select overlapping extensions for the contrastive familiar names (e.g., "spoon" and "fork") as mutually exclusive ones.

The results of the first three experiments have implications for the validity of two methods that have been proposed for analyzing children's productive speech errors. The first is a method proposed by Anglin (1977)

TABLE 11

INTERCORRELATIONS AMONG THE MEASURES OF THE RELATION OF THE TRAINED NAME TO THE TWO OLD NAMES

MEASURES	1	2	3	4	5	6	7	8
ME–referent selection ..	...							
ME–definition	.10[a]	...						
ME–subordination	.12[a]	.43[a,*]	...					
SS–referent selection ...	...	−.03	−.07	...				
SS–definition	−.10	...	−.20	.14[a]	...			
SS–subordination	−.06	.23	...	.16[a]	.21[a]	...		
DS–referent selection ..	...	−.26	−.20	...	−.14	−.34*	...	
DS–definition	−.02	...	−.34*	−.12	...	−.53*	.50[a,*]	...
DS–subordination	−.01	−.41*	...	−.10	−.09	...	.40[a,*]	.63[a,*]

NOTE.—Entries are based on the responses of subjects in the hybrid condition, collapsed over age. ME = mutually exclusive; SS = single ordinate; and DS = double subordinate: for example, ME–referent selection = number of mutually exclusive interpretations based on the rent selection measure.
[a] These nine pairs of measures of the same interpretation were positively correlated.
* $p < .05$, $df = 34$.

for identifying underextensions. He argued that, if a child knows the correct name for something but overextends another name to it, one can infer that the correct name is underextended. For example, if a child knows "truck" but calls a particular truck "car," one can infer that he would not accept "truck" for that truck. The validity of this inference is challenged by the evidence that toddlers often accept more than one name for something. The second method is one suggested by Winner (1979) for distinguishing literal from metaphoric overextensions. According to Winner, if a child calls something by the wrong name but knows its correct name, the usage is metaphoric; otherwise, it is literal. For example, if a child calls a wastebasket "boot" even though she has been heard to say "wastebasket," the usage of "boot" is metaphoric. This kind of inference is also challenged by the evidence that toddlers lack the ME bias. Conversely, the evidence that older children have the bias supports the validity of applying both methods to their speech.

After Early Childhood

In contrast to the 24-month-olds, the older children and adults showed signs of having a moderate ME bias. Both 6- and 19-year-olds showed a significant immediate correction effect but, like the 2½- and 3½-year-olds of experiment 2, they immediately corrected only if the new name's referent was a hybrid rather than a typical referent of the familiar name. This result reflects either subjects' greater certainty that the familiar name denotes the typical or their greater difficulty in perceiving something distinctive about this referent.

The 11-year-olds performed similarly to the 6- and 19-year-olds, but their tendency to immediately correct did not obtain statistical significance. If there is a slight weakening of the ME bias as adolescence approaches, the present study did not have sufficient statistical power to detect it. However, three factors weigh against this possibility. First, the two metalinguistic measures of the bias did not differentiate the 11-year-olds from the 6- and 19-year-olds; in fact, the 11-year-olds were slightly less likely than the other groups to define the hybrid name as a subordinate of the familiar names. Second, the three groups were equally likely to avoid selecting the same drawing as a referent of two familiar names in the test of the restriction effect. Finally, three of the 12 11-year-olds in the hybrid condition showed a consistent immediate correction effect.

It is somewhat surprising that there was no substantial decline in the strength of the immediate correction effect beyond the preschool years. Adults might have been expected to take the introduction of a nonsense word for a picture less seriously than children, and, if so, they should have been less likely to immediately correct. It may have been that some adults did not take the nonsense names seriously when these were introduced for typicals; however, they must have taken them seriously for hybrids—otherwise, they would not have shown the immediate correction effect for these kinds of referents. An adult's decision whether to take a new name seriously (which is the essence of the rejection effect) may depend on how certain she is of another name for its referent. Nevertheless, the finding of an immediate correction effect for hybrids indicates that adults have some kind of ME bias.

Metalinguistic Status of the Bias

How children and adults define new names.—Definitions of the trained names were strikingly different from those that children and adults tend to give for familiar concrete nouns. For example, 6-year-olds almost never and 11-year-olds only occasionally define one familiar noun in terms of another (Norlin, 1981; Watson, 1985). However, the trained name was defined this way on over 90% of the trials. The children's definitions were much more highly structured, in terms of Watson's rule system, than those that they typically supply. Even some of the 6-year-olds' definitions satisfied the most advanced, Aristotelian rule—class name + modification—which is the rule followed in scientific classification systems; however, such definitions were more likely to be supplied by 11- and 19-year-olds. Because input was controlled, this last result indicates that age-related increases in the complexity of definitions are not completely dependent on increases in experience with particular definienda. Children learn a general, productive schema for giving definitions (Watson, 1985), and older children apply it more readily to new words.

The reason for the unusual sophistication of the 6-year-olds' definitions cannot be determined without further research. However, the present results indicate a clear limit on the generalizability of the consistent results of previous studies of children's concrete noun definition. One paradox is that children's definitions are more advanced for recently acquired nouns than for highly familiar ones. It may be important that the children did not receive some types of information about the trained name that they tend to mention in their definitions of familiar names, such as, for instance, functions (Anglin, 1985). It may also be important that the trained name was clearly related to a familiar basic-level name; such names serve as cognitive reference points within noun hierarchies (cf. Mervis & Rosch, 1981). For example, when introducing non-basic-level names to children, adults tend to relate these to basic-level ones explicitly; however, when introducing basic-level names, they do not relate them to other names (Blewitt, 1983; Callanan, 1985). Thus, if children's noun definitions mirror what they have been told about nouns, they should be less likely to define basic-level nouns in terms of other ones than to define the latter (such as the trained names of the present experiment) in terms of the former.

Relations among linguistic and metalinguistic measures.—The effect of object typicality was just as evident in the definitions of trained names as it was in selection of referents for familiar names (which indexed the immediate correction effect). Children were less likely to define the trained name by equating it with a familiar one when it had been introduced for a hybrid. Thus, expression of the ME disposition at the metalinguistic level is also influenced by object typicality.

Anglin (1977) noted that referent selection and definition measures of word knowledge are less consistent for younger than for older children. For example, 5-year-olds may define "food" as "something you can eat" but then fail to pick a piece of candy when asked to select examples of food. Such inconsistency was also evident in the present study; however, 6-, 11-, and 19-year-olds were similarly inconsistent in their responses to questions about names for hybrids (and similarly consistent regarding those for typicals). For example, the referent selection and definition measures of the frequency of ME interpretations by subjects in the hybrid condition were not significantly correlated at any age. Moreover, responses to the subordination questions revealed very little tendency to maintain ME as well as a substantial tendency to allow the trained name to be subordinate to both familiar names.

The finding of inconsistency between different measures of the relation between two extensions is not without precedent. McCloskey and Glucksberg (1978) found that 22% of adults' judgments of the category membership of atypical referents were inconsistent with the judgments they had made a month earlier. Also, Callanan and Markman (1982) and Markman et al. (1980) found substantial inconsistency in two measures of whether children accepted a superordinate name for individuals. As in the present study, one measure was based on referent selections and the other on answers to yes-no questions about one name's semantic relation to another. Given McCloskey & Glucksberg's finding that the categorization of atypicals is inconsistent and Markman's finding that different methods of measurement yield inconsistency, it is not surprising that the present study obtained inconsistency with different measures of the categorization of atypicals. Also, McCloskey and Glucksberg observed that consistency is positively correlated with consensus (between-subject agreement). The inconsistency in the present study was thus somewhat predictable from the nearly complete lack of consensus in judgments by subjects in the hybrid condition regarding the relation between the trained and the familiar names. Consensus and consistency also covaried in the typicals condition—both were high.

The inconsistency of those in the hybrid condition was most likely caused by their uncertainty about how to classify the hybrid. This explanation is incomplete, however, because it does not identify the factors that compel uncertain subjects to change their interpretations. A host of social psychological theories assume that a fundamental human motivation is to avoid inconsistency so as not to create such undesirable impressions as being stupid, weak willed, dishonest, or hypocritical. Even uncertain subjects should stick to their interpretations unless they either forget them or receive additional information. Forgetting could have been responsible for the inconsistency between the referent selection and the two metalinguistic measures since a fair amount of potentially interfering cognitive activity took place between the administration of these measures. Also, the correlations were, in fact, slightly higher between the two metalinguistic measures than between either of these and the linguistic one. However, forgetting could not have been the cause of inconsistency between the metalinguistic measures because these were administered in immediate succession.

The additional information that compelled subjects to revise interpretations may have been pragmatic in nature. Fremgen and Fay (1980) have argued that children may take the repetition of a question to imply the incorrectness of their initial response. In everyday discourse, especially in educational settings, incorrect answers are more likely than correct ones to prompt the repetition of a question. They are also more likely to prompt follow-up questions that focus on the source of error. Thus, some subjects may have reacted to the subordination question (e.g., "Is a bave a kind of car?") as if it indicated a categorization mistake in the definition they had just given for the trained name. Alternatively, the definition, subordination, and referent selection requests may differ in the extent to which they presuppose one kind of semantic relation over another. The subordination question may bias subjects toward the subordinate interpretation because this relation is mentioned in the question ("a kind of"); in fact, this type of question did elicit the greatest number of subordinate interpretations. This hypothesis would also explain why Harris (1975) found 6-year-olds to have a very strong tendency to treat a new name as synonymous with a familiar subordinate name—the children in his study were asked a question that mentioned the synonymy relation (e.g., "Is a mib a bird?"). Clearly, future research could explore these possibilities by posing the questions in different orders, by varying the lag between them, and by posing ones that clearly vary in their presuppositions (e.g., "Is a bave like a car?" or, "Cars and trucks are different kinds of vehicles. Are baves a third kind of vehicle, separate from either cars or trucks?").

VI. EXPERIMENT 4: YOUNG CHILDREN'S JUSTIFICATIONS FOR DISAMBIGUATION

In experiment 2, children as young as 32 months old showed a strong disambiguation effect; that is, they consistently mapped an unfamiliar name to something they could not name rather than to something they could. This effect occurred more reliably than either the immediate correction or the restriction effects. The purpose of the present experiment was to examine whether children who disambiguate would justify their behavior in terms of the ME principle. If so, then we could conclude not only that the ME bias is responsible for disambiguation but also that children are aware of this bias. Justifications are thus a kind of metalinguistic measure.

Children who were either 2½ or 4 years old were given a test identical to the one used in experiment 1, except that they were asked to justify their selections. We predicted that the ME principle would be manifest in behavior before children became aware of it: younger children's selections would be compatible with it, but their justifications would not. The finding that children are not initially aware of a rule that guides their own behavior is frequently obtained in child language research (deVilliers and deVilliers, 1978; Karmiloff-Smith, 1986). For example, children can use many words meaningfully long before they can provide meaningful definitions for them.

A second reason for conducting the present experiment was that the validity of our behavioral measure of disambiguation was not completely beyond doubt. No matter how lengthy the preexposure to novel kinds, one can never be sure that their attraction to them has been sufficiently reduced; older children may still prefer them over old kind–new tokens. Thus, novelty preference, rather than either an ME or a lexical gap–filling bias, could be responsible for the disambiguation effect found in experiments 1 and 2. If some children justified their disambiguation behavior in terms of the ME principle, then we could be more confident that an ME bias, rather than either a novelty preference or a gap-filling bias, is the cause. On the basis of the performance of the preschoolers in the other tests of experiments 1 and 2 as well as in Markman and Wachtel's (1988) and Merriman's (1986b) studies, we expected that the 4-year-olds would tend to justify disambiguation in terms of the ME principle. We did not expect the same for the 2½-year-olds because of the evidence that the principle has only recently begun to influence their behavior and that a considerable lag typically occurs between the linguistic and the metalinguistic expression of a principle.

METHOD

Subjects

Two groups of 18 children, aged, respectively, 2½ years (M = 2-9, range = 2-6–2-11) and 4 years (M = 4-4, range = 4-1–4-7) participated. As before, the children came from middle-class homes and were located through published birth records; each group contained equal numbers of boys and girls.

Materials

Six objects were used—three old kinds (a doll, a key, and a cup) and three new kinds (a clear plastic cube with 12 ball bearings inside, a white ducting tube from a clothes dryer, and a yellow soap dish with a yellow sponge glued into it). A segment of the soap dish was removed so as to give the object an unusual shape.

Procedure

Each child was tested in a lab room by a male experimenter. The experimenter placed the new kinds on a table in front of the child and encouraged her to play with them. After 2 min, the toys were removed, and the child was shown three pairs, each consisting of a new kind–old token (one of the play objects) and an old kind–new token. Before presenting a pair, the experimenter asked, "Do you know what an X is?" where X was an artificial name (either "zav," "danker," or "eisel"). The pairs and names were presented in one of four random orders. After presentation, the child was asked, "Which one is an X? Put your finger on the X." After making a selection, the child was asked, "Why is it an X? How do you know?" The entire procedure was administered in less than 10 min.

RESULTS AND DISCUSSION

The developmental trends obtained in the first two experiments were replicated. The 2½- and the 4-year-olds selected the new kind on 81% and 98% of the trials, respectively. This difference was significant, $t(34) = 2.85$, $p < .01$. Although the toddlers performed well above chance, 10 of 18 selected an old kind on at least one trial. They were also much less likely to admit to being unfamiliar with the new name. They answered "yes" to the question, "Do you know what an X is?" on 52% of the trials, whereas the 4-year-olds did so only 13% of the time. The toddlers were also more likely not to reply at all—40% versus 8% of the trials.

The children's justifications for selecting new kinds over old were assigned to one of three categories: (1) ME—the old kind was named (e.g., "because this is a key"); (2) object property—a property of the new kind was identified (e.g., "It has balls inside"); (3) no response—including responses that did not answer the question (e.g., "I don't know" or "What's this for?"). Justifications that satisfied the criteria for both ME and object property were assigned to the ME category because our purpose was to examine how often children's explanations for their choices clearly implied the ME principle.

ME, object property, and no response constituted 59%, 28%, and 13% of the 4-year-olds' and 10%, 28%, and 62% of the 2½-year-olds' justifications, respectively. The age difference in the tendency to imply the ME principle was significant, $t(34) = 4.73$, $p < .01$. Even if the trials in which children offered no justifications are ignored, the 4-year-olds were more than twice as likely to give ME justifications.

Thus, although most 2½-year-olds tend to select a new kind over an old as the referent of an unfamiliar name, they are only dimly aware of the ME principle. Most of their new kind selections are guided, not by a conscious desire to maintain ME, but by some other psychological force, such as an attraction to novel kinds that is not fully diminished by preexposure, a bias to fill lexical gaps, or an ME bias that is not accessible to consciousness. The results of the immediate correction test of experiment 2 suggest some role for the latter. Awareness of the ME principle must dawn sometime after it begins to influence verbal behavior.

In contrast, 4-year-olds tend to justify their ME-preserving selections in terms of the ME principle, which strongly suggests that these selections are motivated by an ME bias rather than by an attraction to new kinds or a disposition to fill lexical gaps. The results of experiments 1 and 2, as well as those obtained by Markman and Wachtel (1988) and Merriman (1986b), also support the claim that this age group has a substantial ME bias.

VII. GENERAL DISCUSSION

The ME bias has a distinctly different character in each of the following groups—children under 2½ years; those between 2½ and 6 years; and those aged over 6. We will summarize what is known about the bias in each of these groups, then discuss the theoretical implications of this evidence. In the final section, directions for future research will be outlined.

TODDLERS

In Chapter II, we concluded that the evidence was too sparse and contradictory to indicate clearly whether children under age 3 years have any kind of ME bias at all. However, the results of our experiments 1–3 constitute strong support for the claim that children under age 2½ years lack the bias. They consistently failed our tests of disambiguation, immediate correction, and/or restriction. We will discuss the evidence for their failure of each of these tests in turn.

Although Golinkoff et al. (1985) and Vincent-Smith et al. (1974) found 2-year-olds to show a disambiguation effect—that is, a tendency to choose a new kind rather than an old as the referent of an unfamiliar name—it was not clear whether an ME bias accounted for the children's behavior. Two alternative explanations—novelty preference and rapid learning from corrective feedback—could not be ruled out. In experiments 1 and 2, in which a preexposure technique was used to reduce attraction to new kinds and no corrective feedback was given, 24-month-olds showed no disambiguation effect. This result not only suggests the absence of an ME bias but also fails to support Clark's (1987) proposal that toddlers are disposed to fill lexical gaps.

The most confident conclusion of the empirical review presented in Chapter II was that toddlers show no immediate correction effect—contrary to both Barrett's (1978) and Clark's (1983b) claims. The results of experiments 2 and 3 support this conclusion. Toddlers did not immediately correct even when the referent of the new name was an atypical example of a familiar name, that is, even when they should have been somewhat uncertain about the correctness of the familiar name.

Very little research has directly examined the restriction effect in toddlers. The results of experiments 2 and 3 indicated that they fail to show it— they do not avoid generalizing two names to the same referent. In fact, the children were just as likely to select overlapping as mutually exclusive sets of referents for two familiar names from the basic level (e.g., "car" and "truck"). Because it indicates that they will violate ME even with respect to words that have been mutually exclusive in input (i.e., that have never been heard for the same referent), this result strikes a rather strong blow against the ME claim for toddlers. This claim is further challenged by the finding of experiment 3 that toddlers generalize the second name in a test pair just as broadly as the first, even though they overgeneralize the first to what are appropriate referents only of the second. This failure to show even a weak restriction effect is noteworthy because, unlike some of the other ME-based effects, it does not depend on acceptance of adults' authority to teach names; the children only need refrain from accepting a second name for something they themselves have just selected as a referent of another name.

The only empirical leg that the ME claim for toddlers has left to stand on is the evidence that they occasionally reject a new name for an old name's referent (i.e., they show the immediate rejection effect). It is difficult to explain why, if they do have an ME bias, they should show it only in this one way—which, additionally, is counterproductive in that it would hinder word learning. On the other hand, it is also difficult to conceive what factor other than the ME bias could produce this one effect; the following is an attempt to propose such an alternative. First, consider Macnamara's (1982) evidence that 28-month-olds reject superordinate names for individual objects and often justify these rejections by citing familiar basic-level names. Such rejections may not be instances of the immediate rejection effect because the superordinate names may not be unfamiliar; thus, the motivation for rejection may be not to preserve ME but merely to correct a misuse of a familiar name. For example, those who objected to "A piggie is an animal" may have done so not because the statement violated ME but because it was inconsistent with their understanding of "animal." Second, consider the evidence from research by Mervis and her colleagues (Banigan & Mervis, 1988; Mervis, 1984, 1987; Mervis & Canada, 1981) that toddlers resist a new name for an old name's referent if they do not perceive a distinctive property. Children may be opposing not a suggested ME violation in these cases but rather an implicit demand to start calling an object by a new name. A child who believed that something could be called "car" might object to the introduction of "sedan," for example, because she interprets this speech act as indicating that "car" is not the *preferred* name; she infers that the speaker wants her to call it "sedan." The child may not make the stronger inference that the speaker believes "car" is wrong and, because she sees nothing wrong with calling it "car," resists the perceived demand to use the new name.

This explanation fits not only with all the evidence against the ME claim for toddlers but also with another finding reported by Mervis and her colleagues—namely, that if toddlers do perceive a distinctive object property, they will neither reject the new name nor treat it as mutually exclusive with the old one; they will subordinate it. This account is also compatible with the argument developed in Chapter I that the name children prefer to use for something is the one that maps to the category with greatest family resemblance (within- versus between-category similarity). If a distinctive property becomes very salient to a child, the family resemblance that she perceives for the old name's category will be reduced because the level of perceived within-category similarity declines. If this decline is substantial, she may be willing to accept a demand to use the new rather than the old name.

PRESCHOOLERS

We concluded our empirical review in Chapter II by arguing that children aged more than 3 years have a limited ME bias that functions as the default option in their procedures for integrating new and old names. The results of the experiments reported in the four subsequent chapters upheld this argument. In addition, the results of experiment 2 indicate that children as young as 2½ years old have this kind of bias—contrary to Merriman's (1986b) claim. In four studies (Carey & Bartlett, 1978; Merriman, 1986b; and experiments 2 and 3), preschoolers have shown an immediate correction effect. The last three studies cited showed that the size of the effect depends on whether ME-contradictory information is presented in input and on how typical a new name's referent is of an old name's category. Preschoolers have also shown a strong disambiguation effect in four studies, all of which have controlled for novelty preference and for the effects of corrective feedback (Markman & Wachtel, 1988; experiments 1, 2, and 4). Several other studies by Markman and Wachtel indicate that preschoolers' tendency to disambiguate is sometimes, but not always, overridden when placed in conflict with their bias to map new nouns to categories of whole objects. Finally, experiment 2 revealed a strong restriction effect by 3½-year-olds but not by 2½-year-olds.

Most of the evidence indicates that the ME bias grows stronger during the preschool period. In both experiments 1 and 4, 4-year-olds were more likely than younger children both to disambiguate and to acknowledge that a new name was unfamiliar. They were also more likely to justify their disambiguation selections in terms of the ME principle in experiment 4. In

MONOGRAPHS

Merriman's (1986b) study, 6-year-olds showed a greater immediate correction tendency than 4-year-olds, who in turn showed a greater tendency than 2½-year-olds. The results of experiment 2 constitute the only exception to this general age trend; both the disambiguation and the immediate correction tendencies of 2½- and 3½-year-olds were comparable, although the latter group did show a stronger restriction effect.

BEYOND THE PRESCHOOL YEARS

What little evidence there is supports the claim that a default-type ME bias is maintained after the preschool years (Glucksberg & Danks, 1968; Markman et al., 1980; experiment 3). In the third experiment, 6-, 11-, and 19-year-olds showed quite similar tendencies to produce both the immediate correction and the restriction effects under various conditions. Although they showed the first effect only with respect to hybrid referents, they produced the second on nearly every trial in which they selected referents for pairs of familiar nouns from the same basic level (e.g., "spoon" and "fork"). Their patterns of response to metalinguistic questions about these names were also quite similar and indicated an awareness of the ME principle. Although there was some indication that the 11-year-olds might be slightly less likely to maintain ME than either the younger or the older subjects, all three groups generally showed a moderately strong adherence to the ME principle that was sensitive to referent typicality.

THEORETICAL IMPLICATIONS

The empirical evidence has implications for the following issues: how toddlers and older children learn words; the cognitive prerequisites of the ME bias; how nature and nurture affect the bias; the metalinguistic status of the bias; and the timing of the activation of the bias vis-à-vis the acquisition of a new word.

How toddlers learn words.—Because children under age 2½ years lack the bias, they lack a powerful means for avoiding and correcting overextensions. They thus either are considerably prone to overextension or use other means for controlling it. The evidence indicates that there is some truth to both propositions. Toddlers are indeed more likely to overextend than older children (Clark, 1973; Merriman, 1986b; experiments 2 and 3), and it may be no coincidence that very few overextensions are reported in diaries for children aged more than 2½ years (Clark, 1973)—the age at which the ME bias is most likely acquired. On the other hand, their tendency toward overextension (at least in production) is not excessive. In Chapter I, we suggested some factors that might restrict this tendency—children's knowledge of very few referents for any particular word, a tendency for their caregivers to avoid using atypical referents to introduce words, their conservativeness in productive generalization, their knowledge of the implications of input cues for word extension, and their attraction to novel kinds that may prompt the disambiguation effect in natural word learning (where preexposure should rarely occur to reduce such attraction). The results of experiment 1 support this last proposal; toddlers' disambiguation is strongly affected by their attraction to novelty.

We also argued in Chapter I that, even without a bias, young children would eventually start using correct new names instead of overextended old ones because the former were more likely to be better descriptors (i.e., to denote categories with greater within- relative to between-category similarity) and because adults were more likely to model correct usage rather than overextension. The "better descriptor" argument receives indirect support from the finding that toddlers are more likely to accept a new name for the referent of an old name when they perceive a distinctive property (Banigan & Mervis, 1988; Mervis & Canada, 1981). Because they perceive such a property, they should also perceive less similarity between the new and the old words' extensions (lower between-category similarity).

How older children learn words.—Because children aged over 2½ years have the bias, they possess a powerful means for avoiding and correcting overextensions. However, for them the bias should create a problem that it would not for younger children—namely, it should make them prone to underextension (rejecting acceptable word referents). In Chapter I, we argued (*a*) that there may be limits on the bias that serve to minimize this problem and (*b*) that, even if there are not, it is not as serious as the problem of overextension that the bias helps "solve."

As part of argument *a*, we proposed that ME is the default option in older children's procedures for integrating the extensions of new and old names; ME is assumed only if other evidence or biases are not strongly incompatible with it. We argued that the bias will interfere with the acquisition of a new name for an old name's referent only if the person who introduces it lacks credibility, the reference of the introduction is ambiguous, or the referent of the name is an atypical member of the old name's extension. The results of experiments 2 and 3 provide strong support for this argument. When a highly credible experimenter introduced a new name in an unambiguous fashion for a typical member of an old name's extension (e.g., a common fork), children aged over 2½ years showed virtually no tendency to correct the old name or to reject the new one. When the referent was atypical (e.g., a hybrid spoon-fork), however, they tended to correct the old name on approximately half the trials. Anglin (1977) reported a similar effect of typicality on preschoolers' tendency to reject naturally acquired superordinate names for referents of presumably familiar basic-level names.

Another implication of the "default option" position is that older children are sensitive to information in input that contradicts ME even if the contradiction is only suggested. Evidence for such sensitivity can be gleaned from studies by Merriman (1986b), in which older children tended not to correct an old name when properties that its referents shared with those of a new name were emphasized in training, and by Markman et al. (1980), in which older children allowed extensions to overlap when they were told that one name was "a kind of" another. Also, both Harris's (1975) finding that nearly every child who was told that "mib" was a white drink agreed that mib was milk and our observation in experiment 3 that children usually violated ME in response to questions that presupposed the acceptability of such violations may be explicable in terms of children's sensitivity to input that contradicts the ME assumption.

Although various factors limit the severity of the underextension problem for older children, it is not completely eradicated. Callanan and Markman's (1982) results may be representative of the actual extent of the problem. In two studies, 3½-year-olds had some tendency incorrectly to reject superordinate names for individuals; however, they were nearly four times as likely to accept them (79% vs. 21% of the trials). They were even less likely to reject such names for pairs of objects. Thus, although children's superordinate name learning may be impeded by their ME bias, it is unlikely to be drastically impaired.

Our justification for argument *b*—that underextension is not as serious a problem as overextension—was based primarily on the greater prevalence of positive than negative examples in the input to the child. Positive examples are useful for correcting underextension and negative ones for correcting overextension. When informed that something is a positive example of a familiar word, a child should either maintain the word's extension (if it already contains that thing) or expand it (if it does not). Conversely, when informed that something is a negative example, he should either maintain or restrict the extension. Because the child receives input useful for correcting overextension much less frequently than input useful for correcting underextension, it is to his advantage to have a bias that disposes him against overextension, even if it makes him more likely to underextend.

Cognitive prerequisites of the bias.—Our conclusion that the ME bias is not acquired until the preschool years is more compatible with arguments that toddlers lack certain skills necessary for having the bias (Merriman, 1986b; Mervis, 1987) than it is with those that they lack certain skills necessary for overcoming it (Clark, 1983b; Flavell et al., 1986; Markman, 1987).

In Chapter I, we argued that, although toddlers may not think about a thing's membership in one category when they consider whether it belongs to another, they may also have difficulty understanding how something could belong to two categories. It can be argued that all the tests of the bias that we reviewed are sensitive to the first deficit, not to the second. Toddlers who failed the tests of immediate correction and restriction may not have realized that they were selecting overlapping sets of referents. Regarding their failure in tests of the disambiguation effect, however, this argument is difficult to accept. Here, because they often mentioned the familiar name for an object moments before they chose it as the referent of an unfamiliar name, they must have realized that they were assigning two names to the same referent. Although it should be noted that no one has used the strongest test—asking whether some hybrid object is "both an X and a Y"—it is unlikely that toddlers would pass such a test.

The issue of the relation between cognitive ability and the ME bias is far from settled; in fact, no one has established that there is actually any relation at all. The delay in the development of the bias only suggests the possibility of such a relation; it may be that such delay occurs merely because the bias needs to be learned—perhaps from repeated experiences of hearing old names corrected as new names are introduced.

Even if there is a relation, its nature needs to be further specified. Development of the bias could depend on the acquisition of any one, or the combination, of several abilities—thinking about a thing's membership in one category when considering whether it belongs to another, monitoring the extensions of two names for overlap, or perceiving properties that differentiate one category from another. The importance of this last skill is made doubtful by the results of experiments 2 and 3, in which 2-year-olds did not immediately correct even when the referent of the new name was a hybrid that possessed several distinctive properties. Moreover, in Merriman's (1986b) experiment, 2½-year-olds did not immediately correct even when their attention was drawn to distinctive properties. The causal role of the first two abilities we listed is challenged by Taylor and Gelman's (1988) finding that some 2-year-olds generalized a new name for an old name's referent less broadly than one for a new kind of referent. This result could not have been obtained unless the children could coordinate concepts. However, as already argued in Chapter II, not all the 2-year-olds in this study altered their generalization, and the reason may be that some of these children lacked skill in conceptual coordination. Merriman's (1986b) finding that only six of 12 toddlers imposed ME after being told that something "is an X, not a Y," is compatible with this suggestion. (Other suggestions for reconciling Taylor and Gelman's results with the literature on toddlers and the ME bias have been given in Chap. II.)

Finally, it may be that, not only does the development of the bias depend on the acquisition of certain skills, but so does the development of *bias inhibition,* that is, of the ability to override the bias when input clearly signals its inappropriateness. The argument that children have difficulty understanding how something can belong to two categories may be correct, but only for those who can think about relations between categories in the first place. In other words, children might show no tendency to impose ME until they can coordinate concepts, at which point they would show an inflexible ME bias. Later, as they acquire skill at multiple representation, they would become more tolerant of ME violation but still maintain ME as the default relation between extensions. In the studies of multiple representation reported by Flavell et al. (1986), children aged under 3 years were not tested; thus, all the subjects were beyond the age at which the ME bias emerges. Clearly, more research is needed in which children aged 2 years and older are given tests both of the ME bias and of multiple representation (e.g., perspective-taking or appearance-reality differentiation tests).

Nature and nurture.—No strong conclusions can be drawn about the relative roles of nature and nurture in the development of the bias. Nurture arguments are made more tenable by the evidence that the bias is not present at the outset of word learning. However, as already noted, the bias could be an innate principle for organizing relations between extensions that is not accessed until children have sufficient skill at conceptual coordination. Taylor and Gelman's (1988) demonstration that some children have such ability at least 6 months before they manifest an ME bias could be taken to support the argument that, once children start to think about the relations between word extensions, they still need a certain amount of experience with language (e.g., in which old names are corrected as new names are introduced) before they make ME the default relation.

Metalinguistic knowledge.—Experiments 3 and 4 were the first to provide information about the metalinguistic status of the bias. The results of experiment 4 suggest that there is a lag between the point at which children show the disambiguation effect in their selection of referents for unfamiliar names and the time at which they justify these selections in terms of the ME principle. This kind of finding—of metalinguistic knowledge emerging well after its linguistic counterpart—is fairly common in language acquisition research (deVilliers & deVilliers, 1978; Karmiloff-Smith, 1986).

In experiment 3, the metalinguistic measures of 6-, 11-, and 19-year-olds' ME bias yielded results that were in some ways similar and in some ways different from the results for the linguistic measure (referent selection; for a fuller discussion, see Chap. VI). The most striking similarity was in the high level of ME violation when the new name had been introduced for the typical referent of an old name. The most striking dissimilarity occurred when the referent was a hybrid—responses to subordination questions were much more likely to violate ME than were responses to either definition or referent-selection questions. Future research should address the causes of this dissimilarity.

Timing of activation.—The evidence indicates that children over 2½ years occasionally try to impose ME in immediate response to the introduction of a new word but that those under this age do not. One implication is that preschoolers do not delay the imposition of ME until they have become highly familiar with two words, contrary to a claim based on both Karmiloff-Smith's (1986) and MacWhinney's (1987) theories. This claim may be true of children under the age of 2½ years; however, there have been no direct tests to resolve the question. There also have been no tests of whether preschoolers become more likely to impose ME as their familiarity with a pair of words increases. Such tests could be developed rather easily; for example, Merriman's (1986b) successive name-training procedure could be altered so that children of different ages receive several days of training on the second name and then are tested at various intervals for their interpretations of the two names.

DIRECTIONS FOR FUTURE RESEARCH

At various points in this *Monograph*, research lines that might generate useful information regarding unresolved theoretical issues (e.g., timing of activation) have been proposed. In this closing section, we identify two new theoretical issues and describe some studies that would enlighten us about them.

The first is the domain specificity of the bias. The development of many cognitive strategies is known to be domain specific; that is, children apply them to some domains of knowledge well before they apply them to others (Chi, 1978; Keil, 1984). Children may acquire an ME bias for one domain of words before another, and there may be some domains for which the disposition never develops. Gathercole (1987) has suggested that children apply the ME principle to object words prior to applying it to relational ones, but there is not enough evidence to evaluate this proposal. The vast majority of tests of the ME-related effects have involved only object words. Not only are studies that compare object and relational words needed, but so are ones that compare different domains of object words (e.g., names for animate vs. inanimate objects) and different domains of relational words (e.g., names for spatial vs. temporal relations).

Children may impose ME on a level of a semantic field only after they have acquired more than a few names from the field. Prior to it, they may not realize that the particular semantic field exists, that is, that the few words from the field with which they are familiar have referents with common properties. Once the realization that several words belong to the same domain is achieved, they may compare the words' extensions and discover that these are mutually exclusive. The ME rule would then be applied to any new word from the field. These speculations are quite reminiscent of some of Barrett's (1982) proposals about processing stages in young children's object word learning, in which he argued that they must assign two words to a common semantic field before they attempt to abstract contrasts so as to impose ME between them.

The second general issue is whether an ME bias emerges in the development of other cognitive systems in which one set of elements is mapped to another. Counting is one such system: to count correctly, one must adhere to the ME principle by assigning each counting word to one and only one thing in the set being counted. Children do not initially adhere to this principle (Briars & Siegler, 1984; Gelman & Gallistel, 1978). Problems requiring the quantitative comparison of classes (e.g., the Piagetian class inclusion problem) may be particularly interesting because solutions to these will be affected by knowledge both about how to determine word extensions and about how to count. If both types of knowledge are ME biased, this may explain why most children do not solve the class inclusion problem until late in the concrete operational period (Winer, 1980)—its solution requires violating ME not only by allowing two names to share referents but also by counting some objects twice. In fact, Wilkinson (1976) has provided evidence that children's disposition to avoid counting the same thing twice may be responsible for their failures to solve such problems. Findings about the ME bias in word learning may also be useful for explaining children's patterns of response to different class inclusion problems. For example, on the basis of our finding that children are more willing to violate ME when new names are introduced for typical than for atypical referents of other names, one might expect them to be more likely to solve class inclusion problems involving typical rather than atypical subcategories (e.g., "collies" vs. "chihuahuas" in the question, "Are there more dogs or more ———?"). Carson and Abrahamson (1976) have reported just such a result.

Drawing is another mapping system in which children may adopt the ME principle. In drawing, children map a set of forms to a set of flat surfaces, and many preserve ME by not allowing the forms in their drawings to overlap (Goodnow, 1977). If the analogy to noun extension holds, then younger children should be more willing than older ones to tolerate overlaps in their drawings.

Perception of spatial layout is yet another mapping system: objects are assigned by a perceiver to locations in three-dimensional space. By analogy to noun extension, there should be a developmental phase in which an infant fails to realize that two things cannot occupy one space at the same time; observations of babies placing things in their mouths or hands when they already have something in those locations might be taken to support this claim.

Although we suspect that an ME bias is not manifest in the initial stages of the acquisition of any mapping system, it is still possible that the disposition is innate. We have already made this argument for word extension. The structure of the mind may be such that there is a natural tendency to organize mapping systems in this way. There may be a delay before learners realize that they are learning a system, that is, that the different mappings they have learned belong together. Once this is realized, an innate ME principle may be activated.

REFERENCES

Adams, A. K., & Bullock, D. (1986). Apprenticeship in word use: Social convergence processes in learning categorically related nouns. In S. A. Kuczaj & M. D. Barrett (Eds.), *The acquisition of word meaning* (pp. 155–198). New York: Springer.
Anglin, J. M. (1977). *Word, object, and conceptual development.* New York: Norton.
Anglin, J. M. (1985). The child's expressible knowledge of word concepts: What preschoolers can say about the meanings of some nouns and verbs. In K. E. Nelson (Ed.), *Children's language* (Vol. **5,** pp. 77–128). Hillsdale, NJ: Erlbaum.
Banigan, R. L., & Mervis, C. B. (1988). Role of adult input in young children's category evolution: 2. An experimental study. *Journal of Child Language,* **15,** 493–504.
Barrett, M. D. (1978). Lexical development and overextension in child language. *Journal of Child Language,* **5,** 205–219.
Barrett, M. D. (1982). Distinguishing between prototypes: The early acquisition of the meaning of object names. In S. A. Kuczaj (Ed.), *Language development: Vol. 1. Syntax and semantics* (pp. 313–334). Hillsdale: NJ: Erlbaum.
Barrett, M. D. (1986). Early semantic representations and early word usage. In S. A. Kuczaj & M. D. Barrett (Eds.), *The acquisition of word meaning* (pp. 39–67). New York: Springer.
Bartlett, E. J. (1976). Sizing things up: The acquisition of the meaning of dimensional adjectives. *Journal of Child Language,* **3,** 205–219.
Bauer, P. J., & Mandler, J. M. (1989). Taxonomies and triads: Conceptual organization in one- to two-year-olds. *Cognitive Psychology,* **21,** 156–184.
Begg, I., & Denny, P. (1969). Empirical reconciliation of atmosphere and conversion interpretations of syllogistic reasoning errors. *Journal of Experimental Psychology,* **81,** 351–354.
Benedict, H. (1979). Early lexical development: Comprehension and production. *Journal of Child Language,* **6,** 183–200.
Blewitt, P. (1983). *Dog* versus *collie:* Vocabulary in speech to young children. *Developmental Psychology,* **19,** 602–609.
Bowerman, M. (1978). The acquisition of word meaning: An investigation into some current conflicts. In N. Waterson & C. E. Snow (Eds.), *The development of communication* (pp. 263–287). New York: Wiley.
Bowerman, M. (1982). Reorganizational processes in lexical and syntactic development. In E. Wanner & L. R. Gleitman (Eds.), *Language acquisition: The state of the art* (pp. 319–346). London: Cambridge University Press.
Bowerman, M. (1985). Beyond communicative adequacy: From piecemeal knowledge to an integrated system in the child's acquisition of language. In K. E. Nelson (Ed.), *Children's language* (Vol. **5,** pp. 369–398). Hillsdale, NJ: Erlbaum.

Bowerman, M. (1987). Commentary: Mechanisms of language acquisition. In B. MacWhinney (Ed.), *Mechanisms of language acquisition* (pp. 443–466). Hillsdale, NJ: Erlbaum.
Brewer, W. E., & Stone, J. B. (1975). Acquisition of spatial antonym pairs. *Journal of Experimental Child Psychology,* **19,** 299–307.
Briars, D., & Siegler, R. S. (1984). A featural analysis of preschoolers' counting knowledge. *Developmental Psychology,* **20,** 607–618.
Brown, R. (1958). How shall a thing be called? *Psychological Review,* **65,** 14–21.
Brown, R. (1973). *A first language: The early stages.* Cambridge, MA: MIT Press.
Brown, R., & Hanlon, C. (1970). Derivational complexity and order of acquisition in child speech. In J. Hayes (Ed.), *Cognition and the development of language* (pp. 11–53). New York: Wiley.
Callanan, M. A. (1985). How parents label objects for young children: The role of input in the acquisition of category hierarchies. *Child Development,* **56,** 508–523.
Callanan, M. A., & Markman, E. M. (1982). Principles of organization in young children's natural language hierarchies. *Child Development,* **53,** 1093–1101.
Carey, S. (1978). The child as word learner. In M. Halle, J. Bresnan, & G. A. Miller (Eds.), *Linguistic theory and psychological reality* (pp. 264–293). Cambridge, MA: MIT Press.
Carey, S., & Bartlett, E. J. (1978). Acquiring a single new word. *Papers and Reports on Child Language,* **15,** 17–29.
Carson, M. T., & Abrahamson, A. (1976). Some members are more equal than others: The effects of semantic typicality on class-inclusion performance. *Child Development,* **47,** 1186–1190.
Case, R. (1985). *Intellectual development: A systematic reinterpretation.* New York: Academic.
Chambers, J. C., & Tavuchis, N. (1976). Kids and kin: Children's understanding of American kin terms. *Journal of Child Language,* **3,** 62–80.
Chi, M. T. H. (1978). Knowledge structure and memory development. In R. S. Siegler (Ed.), *Children's thinking: What develops?* (pp. 73–96). Hillsdale, NJ: Erlbaum.
Chomsky, N. (1959). A review of B. F. Skinner's *Verbal Behavior. Language,* **35,** 26–58.
Clark, E. V. (1973). What's in a word? On the child's acquisition of semantics in his first language. In T. E. Moore (Ed.), *Cognitive development and the acquisition of language* (pp. 65–110). New York: Academic.
Clark, E. V. (1983a). Convention and contrast in acquiring the lexicon. In T. B. Seiler & W. Wannenmacher (Eds.), *Concept development and the development of word meaning* (pp. 67–89). New York: Springer.
Clark, E. V. (1983b). Meanings and concepts. In J. H. Flavell & E. M. Markman (Eds.), P. H. Mussen (Series Ed.), *Handbook of child psychology: Vol. 3. Cognitive development* (pp. 787–840). New York: Wiley.
Clark, E. V. (1987). The principle of contrast: A constraint on language acquisition. In B. MacWhinney (Ed.), *Mechanisms of language acquisition* (pp. 1–34). Hillsdale, NJ: Erlbaum.
Clark, E. V. (1988). On the logic of contrast. *Journal of Child Language,* **15,** 317–335.
Clark, R. (1980). Errors in talking to learn. *First Language,* **1,** 7–32.
Collis, G. M. (1977). Visual co-orientation and maternal speech. In H. R. Schaffer (Ed.), *Studies in mother-infant interaction* (pp. 355–378). New York: Academic.
Cruse, D. A. (1977). A note on the learning of colour names. *Journal of Child Language,* **4,** 305–311.
DeMarie-Dreblow, D., & Miller, P. H. (1988). The development of children's strategies for selective attention: Evidence for a transitional period. *Child Development,* **59,** 1504–1513.

de Villiers, J. G., & de Villiers, P. A. (1978). *Language acquisition.* Cambridge, MA: Harvard University Press.
Dockrell, J., & Campbell, R. (1986). Lexical acquisition strategies in the preschool child. In S. A. Kuczaj & M. D. Barrett (Eds.), *The acquisition of word meaning* (pp. 121–154). New York: Springer.
Donaldson, M., & Wales, P. J. (1970). On the acquisition of some relational terms. In J. R. Hayes (Ed.), *Cognition and the development of language* (pp. 235–268). New York: Wiley.
Elkind, D. (1961). The child's conception of his religious denomination: 1. The Jewish child. *Journal of Genetic Psychology,* **99,** 209–225.
Elkind, D. (1962). The child's conception of his religious denomination: 2. The Catholic child. *Journal of Genetic Psychology,* **101,** 185–193.
Faulkender, P. J., Wright, J. C., & Waldron, A. (1974). Generalized habituation of conceptual stimuli in toddlers. *Child Development,* **45,** 351–356.
Fischer, K. W. (1980). A theory of cognitive development: The control and construction of hierarchies of skills. *Psychological Review,* **87,** 477–531.
Flavell, J. H., Green, F. L., & Flavell, E. R. (1986). Development of knowledge about the appearance-reality distinction. *Monographs of the Society for Research in Child Development,* **51**(1, Serial No. 212).
Fodor, J. D., & Crain, S. (1987). Simplicity and generality of rules in language acquisition. In B. MacWhinney (Ed.), *Mechanisms of language acquisition* (pp. 35–64). Hillsdale, NJ: Erlbaum.
Fremgen, A., & Fay, D. (1980). Overextensions in production and comprehension: A methodological clarification. *Journal of Child Language,* **7,** 205–211.
Gathercole, V. C. (1979). *Birdies like birdseed the bester than buns: A study of relational comparatives and their acquisition.* Unpublished doctoral dissertation, University of Kansas.
Gathercole, V. C. (1987). The contrastive hypothesis for the acquisition of word meaning: A reconsideration of the theory. *Journal of Child Language,* **14,** 493–532.
Gelman, R., & Gallistel, C. R. (1978). *The child's understanding of number.* Cambridge, MA: Harvard University Press.
Gelman, S. A., & Taylor, M. (1984). How two-year-old children interpret proper and common names for unfamiliar objects. *Child Development,* **55,** 1535–1540.
Glucksberg, S., & Danks, J. H. (1968). Effects of discriminative labels and of nonsense labels upon availability of novel function. *Journal of Verbal Learning and Verbal Behavior,* **7,** 72–76.
Goldin-Meadow, S., Seligman, M. E. P., & Gelman, R. (1976). Language in the two-year-old. *Cognition,* **4,** 189–202.
Golinkoff, R. M., Hirsh-Pasek, K., Baduini, C., & Lavallee, A. (1985, April). *What's in a word? The young child's predisposition to use lexical contrast.* Paper presented at the Boston University Conference on Language Development, Boston.
Goodman, N. (1972). *Problems and projects.* Indianapolis: Bobbs-Merrill.
Goodnow, J. (1977). *Children drawing.* Cambridge, MA: Harvard University Press.
Gruendel, J. (1977). Referential extension in early language development. *Child Development,* **48,** 1567–1576.
Harris, P. (1975). Inferences and semantic development. *Journal of Child Language,* **2,** 143–152.
Haviland, S. E., & Clark, E. V. (1974). "This man's father is my father's son": A study of the acquisition of English kin terms. *Journal of Child Language,* **1,** 23–48.
Jacoby, L. L., & Craik, F. I. M. (1979). Effects of elaboration of processing at encoding and retrieval: Trace distinctiveness and recovery of initial context. In L. S. Cermak &

F. I. M. Craik (Eds.), *Levels of processing in human memory* (pp. 1–22). Hillsdale, NJ: Erlbaum.
Just, M. A., & Carpenter, P. A. (1987). *The psychology of reading and language comprehension.* Boston: Allyn & Bacon.
Karmiloff-Smith, A. (1979). *A functional approach to child language.* Cambridge: Cambridge University Press.
Karmiloff-Smith, A. (1986). From meta-processes to conscious access: Evidence from children's metalinguistic and repair data. *Cognition,* **23,** 95–147.
Katz, N., Baker, E., & Macnamara, J. (1974). What's in a name? A study of how children learn common and proper nouns. *Child Development,* **45,** 469–473.
Keil, F. C. (1984). Mechanisms in cognitive development and the structure of knowledge. In R. J. Sternberg (Ed.), *Mechanisms of cognitive development* (pp. 81–100). New York: Freeman.
Kemler, D. (1983). Holistic and analytic modes in perceptual and cognitive development. In T. J. Tighe & B. E. Shepp (Eds.), *Perception, cognition, and development: Interactional analyses* (pp. 77–102). Hillsdale, NJ: Erlbaum.
Kendler, H. H., & Guenther, K. (1980). Developmental changes in classificatory behavior. *Child Development,* **51,** 339–348.
Kuczaj, S. A. (1975). On the acquisition of a semantic system. *Journal of Verbal Learning and Verbal Behavior,* **14,** 340–358.
Kuczaj, S. A. (1977). The acquisition of regular and irregular past tense forms. *Journal of Verbal Learning and Verbal Behavior,* **16,** 589–600.
Kuczaj, S. A. (1982). Children's overextensions in comprehension and production: Support for a prototype theory of object word meaning acquisition. *First Language,* **3,** 93–105.
Kuczaj, S. A., & Lederberg, A. (1977). Height, age, and function: Differing influences on children's comprehension of *younger* and *older. Journal of Child Language,* **4,** 395–416.
Labov, W. (1973). The boundaries of words and their meanings. In C-J. N. Bailey & R. Shuy (Eds.), *New ways of analyzing variation in English.* Washington, DC: Georgetown University Press.
Leopold, W. P. (1939). *Speech development of a bilingual child: A linguist's record: Vol. 1. Vocabulary growth in the first two years.* Evanston, Ill.: Northwestern University Press.
Leopold, W. P. (1949). *Speech development of a bilingual child: A linguist's record: Vol. 3. Grammar and general problems in the first two years.* Evanston, Ill.: Northwestern University Press.
Lewis, M. M. (1951). *Infant speech: A study of the beginnings of language.* New York: Humanities.
Litowitz, B. (1977). Learning to make definitions. *Journal of Child Language,* **4,** 289–304.
Lucariello, J., & Nelson, K. (1986). Context effects on lexical specificity in maternal and child discourse. *Journal of Child Language,* **13,** 507–522.
Lyons, J. (1977). *Semantics 1.* London: Cambridge University Press.
McCloskey, M. E., & Glucksberg, S. (1978). Natural categories: Well-defined or fuzzy sets? *Memory and Cognition,* **6,** 462–472.
Macnamara, J. (1982). *Names for things: A study of human learning.* Cambridge, MA: MIT Press.
Macnamara, J. (1986). *A border dispute: The place of logic in psychology.* Cambridge, MA: MIT Press.
McShane, J. (1980). *Learning to talk.* Cambridge: Cambridge University Press.
MacWhinney, B. (1987). The competition model. In B. MacWhinney (Ed.), *Mechanisms of language acquisition* (pp. 249–308). Hillsdale, NJ: Erlbaum.

MONOGRAPHS

Markman, E. M. (1981). Comprehension monitoring. In W. P. Dickson (Ed.), *Children's oral communication skills* (pp. 61–84). New York: Academic.

Markman, E. M. (1984). The acquisition and hierarchical organization of categories by children. In C. Sophian (Ed.), *Origins of cognitive skills* (pp. 371–406). Hillsdale, NJ: Erlbaum.

Markman, E. M. (1987). How children constrain the possible meanings of words. In U. Neisser (Ed.), *Concepts and conceptual development: Ecological and intellectual factors in categorization* (pp. 255–287). Cambridge: Cambridge University Press.

Markman, E. M., Horton, M. S., & McLanahan, A. G. (1980). Classes and collections: Principles of organization in the learning of hierarchical relations. *Cognition*, **8**, 227–242.

Markman, E. M., & Hutchinson, J. E. (1984). Children's sensitivity to constraints on word meaning: Taxonomic vs. thematic relations. *Cognitive Psychology*, **16**, 1–27.

Markman, E. M., & Wachtel, G. F. (1988). Children's use of mutual exclusivity to constrain the meanings of words. *Cognitive Psychology*, **20**, 121–157.

Medin, D. L. (1983). Structural principles in categorization. In T. J. Tighe & B. E. Shepp (Eds.), *Perception, cognition, and development: Interactional analyses* (pp. 203–230). Hillsdale, NJ: Erlbaum.

Merriman, W. E. (1984, October). *Change in word meaning induced by the acquisition of a new word: A developmental study.* Paper presented at the Boston University Conference on Language Development, Boston.

Merriman, W. E. (1986a). How children learn the reference of concrete nouns: A critique of current hypotheses. In S. A. Kuczaj & M. D. Barrett (Eds.), *The acquisition of word meaning* (pp. 1–38). New York: Springer.

Merriman, W. E. (1986b). Some reasons for the occurrence and eventual correction of children's naming errors. *Child Development*, **57**, 942–952.

Merriman, W. E. (1987, April). *Lexical contrast in toddlers: A reanalysis of the diary evidence.* Paper presented at the biennial meeting of the Society for Research in Child Development, Baltimore.

Merriman, W. E., & Bowman, L. L. (1987, April). *Developmental studies of lexical contrast.* Paper presented at the biennial meeting of the Society for Research in Child Development, Baltimore.

Merriman, W. E., & Koshmider, J. W. (1987, June). *A developmental study of the effect of exemplar information on name generalization.* Paper presented at the symposium of the Jean Piaget Society, Philadelphia.

Mervis, C. B. (1984). Early lexical development: The contributions of mother and child. In C. Sophian (Ed.), *Origins of cognitive skills* (pp. 339–370). Hillsdale, NJ: Erlbaum.

Mervis, C. B. (1987). Child-basic object categories and early lexical development. In U. Neisser (Ed.), *Concepts and conceptual development: Ecological and intellectual factors in categorization* (pp. 201–233). Cambridge: Cambridge University Press.

Mervis, C. B., & Canada, K. (1981, March). *Child-basic categories and early lexical development.* Paper presented at the biennial meeting of the Society for Research in Child Development, Boston.

Mervis, C. B., & Canada, K. (1983). On the existence of competence errors in early comprehension: A reply to Fremgen and Fay and Chapman and Thomson. *Journal of Child Language*, **10**, 431–440.

Mervis, C. B., & Mervis, C. A. (1982). Leopards are kitty-cats: Object labeling by mothers for their thirteen-month-olds. *Child Development*, **53**, 267–273.

Mervis, C. B., & Pani, J. R. (1980). Acquisition of basic object categories. *Cognitive Psychology*, **12**, 496–522.

Mervis, C. B., & Rosch, E. (1981). Categorization of natural objects. In M. R. Rosenzweig & L. W. Porter (Eds.), *Annual Review of Psychology* (Vol. 32, pp. 89–115). Palo Alto, CA: Annual Reviews.
Messer, D. J. (1978). The integration of mother's referential speech with joint play. *Child Development,* **49,** 781–787.
Nelson, K. (1973). Structure and strategy in learning to talk. *Monographs of the Society for Research in Child Development,* 38(1–2, Serial No. 149).
Nelson, K. (1974). Concept, word, and sentence: Interrelations in acquisition and development. *Psychological Review,* **81,** 267–285.
Nelson, K. (1979). Features, contrasts, and the FCH: Some comments on Barrett's lexical development hypothesis. *Journal of Child Language,* **6,** 139–146.
Nelson, K. (1988). Constraints on word learning? *Cognitive Development,* **3,** 221–246.
Nelson, K. E., & Bonvillian, J. D. (1973). Concepts and words in the two-year-old: Acquisition of concept names under controlled conditions. *Cognition,* **2,** 435–450.
Nelson, K. E., & Bonvillian, J. D. (1978). Early language development: Conceptual growth and related processes between 2 and 4½ years. In K. E. Nelson (Ed.), *Children's language* (Vol. **1,** pp. 467–556). New York: Gardner.
Nelson, K. E., & Nelson, K. (1978). Cognitive pendulums and their linguistic realization. In K. E. Nelson (Ed.), *Children's language* (Vol. **1,** pp. 223–285). New York: Gardner.
Ninio, A. (1980). Ostensive definition in vocabulary teaching. *Journal of Child Language,* **7,** 565–573.
Norlin, P. F. (1981). The development of relational arcs in the lexical semantic memory structures of young children. *Journal of Child Language,* **8,** 385–402.
Nystrand, M. (1982). *What writers know: The language, process, and structure of written discourse.* New York: Academic.
Oviatt, S. L. (1980). The emerging ability to comprehend language: An experimental approach. *Child Development,* **51,** 97–106.
Pavlovitch, M. (1920). *Le langage enfantin: Acquisition du serbe et du francais par un enfant serbe.* Paris: Champion.
Piaget, J. (1928). *Judgment and reasoning in the child.* London: Routledge & Kegan Paul.
Piaget, J. (1970). Piaget's theory. In P. H. Mussen (Ed.), *Carmichael's manual of child psychology* (Vol. **1,** pp. 703–733). New York: Wiley.
Ravn, K. E., & Gelman, S. A. (1984). Rule usage in children's understanding of "big" and "little." *Child Development,* **55,** 2141–2150.
Reich, P. A. (1976). The early acquisition of word meaning. *Journal of Child Language,* **3,** 117–123.
Rescorla, L. A. (1976). *Concept formation in word learning.* Unpublished doctoral dissertation, Yale University.
Rescorla, L. A. (1980). Overextension in early language development. *Journal of Child Language,* **7,** 321–335.
Richards, M. M. (1976). Come and go reconsidered: Children's use of deictic verbs in contrived situations. *Journal of Verbal Learning and Verbal Behavior,* **15,** 655–665.
Richards, M. M. (1979). Sorting out what's in a word from what's not: Evaluating Clark's semantic features acquisition theory. *Journal of Experimental Child Psychology,* **27,** 1–47.
Rosch, E. H., Mervis, C. B., Gray, W., Johnson, D., & Boyes-Braem, P. (1976). Basic objects in natural categories. *Cognitive Psychology,* **8,** 382–439.
Rosch, E. H., Simpson, C., & Miller, R. S. (1976). Structural bases of typicality effects. *Journal of Experimental Psychology: Human Perception and Performance,* **2,** 491–502.
Ruke-Dravina, V. (1959). On the emergence of inflection in child language: A contribution based on Latvian speech data. *International Journal of Slavic Linguistics and Poetics,* **1/2,** 201–222.

Schmidt, C. R., & Shatz, M. (1986). Development of conventional object term descriptions. *Developmental Psychology*, **22**, 557–561.

Shipley, E. F., Kuhn, I., & Madden, E. C. (1983). Mothers' use of superordinate category terms. *Journal of Child Language*, **10**, 571–588.

Sigel, I. E., Saltz, E., & Roskind, W. (1967). Variables determining concept conservation in children. *Journal of Experimental Psychology*, **74**, 471–475.

Skinner, B. F. (1957). *Verbal Behavior*. New York: Appleton-Century-Crofts.

Sugarman, S. (1982). Transitions in early representational intelligence: Changes over time in children's productions of simple block structures. In G. E. Forman (Ed.), *Action and thought: From sensorimotor structures to symbolic operations* (pp. 65–93). New York: Academic.

Sugarman, S. (1987). Young children's spontaneous inspection of negative instances in a search task. *Journal of Experimental Child Psychology*, **44**, 170–191.

Taylor, M., & Gelman, S. A. (1988). Adjectives and nouns: Children's strategies for learning new words. *Child Development*, **59**, 411–419.

Templin, M. (1957). *Certain language skills in children: Their development and interrelationship*. Minneapolis: University of Minnesota Press.

Thomson, J., & Chapman, R. W. (1977). Who is "Daddy" revisited: The status of two-year-olds' overextended words in use and comprehension. *Journal of Child Language*, **4**, 359–375.

Vincent-Smith, L., Bricker, D., & Bricker, W. (1974). Acquisition of receptive vocabulary in the toddler-age child. *Child Development*, **45**, 189–193.

Watson, R. (1985). Towards a theory of definition. *Journal of Child Language*, **12**, 181–197.

Wehren, A., DeLisi, R., & Arnold, M. (1981). The development of noun definition. *Journal of Child Language*, **8**, 165–175.

White, T. G. (1982). Naming practices, typicality, and underextension in child language. *Journal of Experimental Child Psychology*, **33**, 324–346.

Whitehurst, G. J., Kedesdy, J., & White, T. G. (1982). A functional analysis of meaning. In S. A. Kuczaj (Ed.), *Language development: Vol. 1. Syntax and semantics* (pp. 397–428). Hillsdale, NJ: Erlbaum.

Wilkinson, A. (1976). Counting strategies and semantic analyses as applied to class inclusion. *Cognitive Psychology*, **8**, 64–85.

Winer, G. A. (1980). Class-inclusion reasoning in children: A review of the empirical literature. *Child Development*, **51**, 309–328.

Winner, E. (1979). New names for old things: The emergence of metaphoric language. *Journal of Experimental Child Psychology*, **6**, 469–492.

Yussen, S. R., & Levy, V. M. (1975). Developmental changes in predicting one's own span of short-term memory. *Journal of Experimental Child Psychology*, **19**, 502–508.

ACKNOWLEDGMENTS

This research was partially supported by a summer research grant from Kent State University. We are grateful to the children, parents, and staff associated with Children's Village of Kent, Gerber Children's Center of Stow, Grace Baptist Church of Kent, Ravenna Christian Academy, and the Institute of Child Development of the University of Minnesota. We thank Michelle Zink for assistance in data collection. The helpful comments of two anonymous reviewers were greatly appreciated. "In all your ways acknowledge Him, and He will make your paths straight" (Prov. 3:6). Address all correspondence to the authors at Department of Psychology, Kent State University, Kent, OH 44242.

COMMENTARY

MAKING WORDS MAKE SENSE

BRIAN MAC WHINNEY

When I use a word, it means just what I choose it to mean—neither more nor less. [Humpty-Dumpty to Alice in Lewis Carroll's *Through the Looking Glass*]

This *Monograph* makes a major contribution to our understanding of a crucial aspect of the transition from infancy to childhood—the transition in which the child learns to make sense of the vast system of categories formalized in every human language. When faced with the task of deciphering a complex code, one always looks for a Rosetta stone. In the area of word learning, Markman (1984) has suggested that the child's Rosetta stone for word learning might well be the notion of mutual exclusivity (ME). But Markman's proposal is not the only one in the field. Other rich and compelling ways of viewing the process of conceptual development focus on the roles of hierarchies, contrasts, strategies, competitions, innate predispositions, regularity in input, and parental guidance. In a masterful fashion, Merriman and Bowman guide the reader through this bewildering forest of ideas, paying close attention to the signposts marked out by the empirical facts. Having laid down this rich conceptual analysis, they then go on to present three of the most carefully designed studies to be found in this literature. Their *Monograph* stands as the most clear-sighted view of this area of child development that has yet been published. It contributes in significant ways to one of the most important current discussions in the field.

The problem of ME is no new issue to philosophical and linguistic discussions of word meaning. That great rational philosopher Humpty-Dumpty elucidated parts of this problem when he declared that, when it comes to dealing with words, one simply has to show them who is to be master. In a sense, the various currents feeding into the ME bias all represent attempts to gain Humpty-Dumpty-like mastery over the possible meanings of words. However, for the young child, this "take control" approach to language does not come so easily. The toddler is a trusting creature who tends to treat parents as the source of all wisdom. The child would prefer simply to use words the way that parents do. In fact, Merriman and Bowman argue that this may indeed be what happens at first. Yet, eventually, the serpent of error intrudes on the trusting relation between children and their parents. Sooner or later, children realize that there is some mismatch between what their parents intended and what they thought their parents intended. The problem is that it is hard for the child to know exactly how the parent intends for each word to be used. Parents do not provide instructions on how to use the words they teach. Nor do words come equipped with their own instructions. Not even the most cautious parent can foresee all the ways that a new word will be interpreted. Thus, inevitably, the child has to adopt an active stance in the task of word learning. Children must begin to find limits that shape the possible ways in which they can interpret new words. Where the parent's limits fail, children have to learn to set their own limits.

This is where ME fits in. Merriman and Bowman argue convincingly that the ME bias does not govern the toddler's first attempts at word learning. Instead, its influence grows slowly over time. Merriman and Bowman define the bias in a few simple words as a disposition "to keep the set of referents of one word from overlapping with those of others" (p. v). They are quite careful never to speak of this bias or disposition as a "constraint." Although it may not be the case that an inexhaustible array of hypotheses drives children into the waiting arms of a strong inborn ME constraint, one still needs to provide some alternative account of how children home in on the correct relations while avoiding the myriad possible wrong interpretations of words. Here, Merriman and Bowman opt for the most reasonable alternative. Rather than relying on a strong early ME constraint, they choose to emphasize the conservative nature of the young child's approach to word learning. They point out that, without this conservativism, a child who knows only two words would use them as if they were yin and yang, dividing the universe between the light and the dark. Of course, nothing of the sort happens. Some early words have wide ranges of reference; others have narrow scopes. But the same can be said for adult word meanings. It is true that some parent psycholinguists, such as Mervis (1984) or Leopold (1939), have detected large numbers of overgeneralizations in the speech of their children. But many of these overgeneralizations can be traced to inconsistencies in the adult input. Still other parent psycholinguists, such as Macnamara (1982) and MacWhinney (1984), have found that their children picked up new words with a startlingly small number of overgeneralization errors. In such cases, it appears that the input was clear and consistent. In general, the child seems to be adept at mirroring the statistical configuration of the input. Thus, there seems to be good empirical support for the view of the child as a conservative word learner.

Merriman and Bowman never tell us exactly how it is that the toddler manages to maintain a conservative interpretation of the input. However, it would seem that their analysis is most consistent with some instance-based model of word learning. In a model of this type, the extension of each word is precisely the set of objects for which the child has actual empirical evidence that a word was used. According to this view, the child's memory for the referent of a new word could be extremely detailed. Hearing the word "cookies" used when the mother is transferring some newly baked cookies into a cookie jar, the child could initially form an association between "cookies" and the act of transfer, the presence of a cookie jar, the shapes of the cookies, the heat coming from the oven door, and the smell of the cookies. Subsequent uses of the word "cookies" would eliminate much of this episodic detail, leaving a core nominal referent. One might argue that expecting a toddler to have this kind of veridical memory for instances may be asking too much. But one must remember that, although the toddler's memory may not be sharply categorized, it is nonetheless extremely flexible. According to this view, the most likely way that a child could avoid building cognition on top of the ME constraint would be to build cognition on top of a powerful memory.

Disambiguation, Correction, and Rejection

The most remarkable contribution of the Merriman and Bowman *Monograph* is the evidence it provides for the development of the ME constraint during the third year. Merriman and Bowman do an excellent job of turning the argument for an innate ME bias on its head. Having shown that the young child can learn without relying on this bias, they then go on to show how important the bias is for the older child. There are two arguments here. The empirical argument focuses on a set of three strategies the child can use to maintain ME when confronted with a new name. These are the strategies of *disambiguation, correction,* and *rejection*. Merriman and Bowman distinguish a subcase of correction that they call *restriction*. However, because it is fairly difficult to separate restriction from correction in actual practice, it may be easier at first glance to think of the two strategies as involving a single basic process. The core contribution of both the analytic and empirical work in this *Monograph* is the construction of a clear understanding of how the child uses these three strategies when confronted with new words. Consider the case of a child who knows the word "cup" but not the word "demitasse." If a child is using the ME bias, we would expect to find either (1) that, when the child sees both a demitasse and a prototypical cup and is asked to bring "the demitasse," she will bring the demitasse (disambiguation); (2) that, when the child is told that a particular cup is a "demitasse," she will decide that it is wrong to call it a "cup" (correction); or (3) that, when the child is told that a particular cup is a "demitasse," she will respond, "No, cup" (rejection).

Why Do Children Develop These Strategies?

Each of these three strategies can be seen as serving a useful purpose in acquisition, quite apart from their possible role in enforcing ME. The disambiguation strategy provides the child with a good guess about what a new word might mean. As a child's vocabulary increases, it becomes increasingly likely that disambiguation will be useful since there are fewer and fewer objects without names. The rejection strategy functions most effectively as a way of requesting disambiguation from the parent. If the child says, "No, cup," the parent can go on and explain to the child how a demitasse differs from other cups.

Of these three strategies, the correction strategy is the most important. Correction works to prune back overgeneralizations that may have occurred during the process of word learning. For the younger child, the rich episodic basis for words may block their excessive overgeneralization. But, for the older child, it may become increasingly costly to maintain such an episodic data base. If the child can properly coordinate the correction strategy with other strategies that support the construction of subordinate and superordinate classes, it may not be necessary to continue to maintain the full set of referents underlying each word. A child should not apply the correction strategy to "demitasse" and "cup" unless it is clear that "demitasse" is not subordinate to "cup," or vice versa. However, if there is no evidence for subordinate or superordinate relations, the child can proceed to correct the referential scope of the word "cup."

Competition versus Strategy

The general view that Merriman and Bowman are developing is one that I find quite convincing. As children grow older, the linguistic problems that they confront become more complex, and they develop more complex ways of dealing with these problems. However, it seems to me that these additional strategies must be viewed as overlays on a basic process of lexical acquisition that is working against a backdrop of competitions between words for references. Competition is not a linguistic constraint but a basic characteristic of the human information-processing system. Competition makes it so that, if a referent is repeatedly called a "demitasse," the association between the word and the referent will grow in strength. This allows it to compete successfully in the relevant instances with the word "cup." Merriman and Bowman fault the competition model approach for not providing an explanation for the development of the correction strategy in 3- and 4-year-olds. But it seems to me that the correction strategy is entirely compatible with the attempt to minimize competition between forms envisaged by the competition model. Merriman and Bowman are correct in claiming that this is a strategy, not an inborn constraint. However, it seems to me that use of the correction strategy can be directly motivated by competition between words.

How might this work? Consider what happens during a particular experiment in which a child may acquire episodic information that links the word "demitasse" to a small teacup. The new form "demitasse" is a very precise word with an extremely limited semantic range. The old form "cup," on the other hand, is a fairly general word with a much broader semantic range. The information-processing framework of the competition model specifies that, when a specific accurate match competes against a less specific match, the more specific match will dominate if it is accurate. Thus, specificity would bar application of "cup" as a name for the demitasse during the episode of learning. However, the competition model would assume that this particular effect would fade over time outside the domain of the experiment. When the child confronts a new demitasse in a second, radically different situation, the word "demitasse" will compete with the word "cup." If the adult again provides the name "demitasse," the child will be further induced to carve out part of the territory of the word "cup" for the new word "demitasse." The competition model claim is that the "correction" made during the course of these experiences is permanent only to the degree that it is further supported by later experiences.

Whither the ME bias?

Merriman and Bowman show how the ME bias has analogues in areas as diverse as drawing and counting. I much agree that basic cognitive principles such as the ME constraint should have an effect throughout cognition. The extension of the concept across such domains will certainly be an interesting fallout from this line of research. However, I doubt that ME itself will be able to support generalizations of this type. The notion of ME has served a useful function as a rallying point motivating studies of conceptual developments during the transition from infancy to childhood. However, as Merriman and Bowman have shown, ME is not a fundamental constraint but a set of learned assumptions that allow us to process new words and new relations more quickly. It is time now for the study of ME to give way to a more detailed process-based account of early word learning. At the same time, any more detailed model must continue to provide us with an understanding of the ways in which the child, like Humpty-Dumpty, learns to control the world rather than being controlled by it.

References

Leopold, W. P. (1939). *Speech development of a bilingual child: A linguist's record: Vol. 1. Vocabulary growth in the first two years.* Evanston, Ill.: Northwestern University Press.
Macnamara, J. (1982). *Names for things: A study of human learning.* Cambridge, MA: MIT Press.
MacWhinney, B. (1984). Where do categories come from? In C. Sophian (Ed.), *Origins of cognitive skills.* Hillsdale, NJ: Erlbaum.
Markman, E. M. (1984). The acquisition and hierarchical organization of categories by children. In C. Sophian (Ed.), *Origins of cognitive skills* (pp. 371–406). Hillsdale, NJ: Erlbaum.
Mervis, C. B. (1984). Early lexical development: The contributions of mother and child. In C. Sophian (Ed.), *Origins of cognitive skills* (pp. 339–370). Hillsdale, NJ: Erlbaum.

CONTRIBUTORS

William E. Merriman (Ph.D. 1984, University of Minnesota) is assistant professor of psychology at Kent State University. His research has focused on developmental change in language and memory in early childhood and on individual differences in intelligence in older children and adults. He recently received a First Independent Research Support and Transition Award from the National Institute of Child Health and Human Development (1 R29 HD25958-O1) that will support five years of further research on the mutual exclusivity bias in children's word learning.

Laura L. Bowman (Ph.D. 1989, Kent State University) is visiting assistant professor at Central Connecticut State University. Her research interests include young children's word meaning acquisition and adults' memory processes.

Brian MacWhinney (Ph.D. 1975, University of California, Berkeley) is professor of psychology at Carnegie-Mellon University. His work on language acquisition has focused on two main areas of research: computational modeling, particularly of the acquisition of syntax and morphology, and the cross-linguistic study of the acquisition of sentence-processing strategies. Among his publications is "The Acquisition of Morphophonology," *Monographs of the Society for Research in Child Development*, Vol. 43, Nos. 1–2, Serial No. 174, 1978.

STATEMENT OF EDITORIAL POLICY

The *Monographs* series is intended as an outlet for major reports of developmental research that generate authoritative new findings and use these to foster a fresh and/or better-integrated perspective on some conceptually significant issue or controversy. Submissions from programmatic research projects are particularly welcome; these may consist of individually or group-authored reports of findings from some single large-scale investigation or of a sequence of experiments centering on some particular question. Multiauthored sets of independent studies that center on the same underlying question can also be appropriate; a critical requirement in such instances is that the various authors address common issues and that the contribution arising from the set as a whole be both unique and substantial. In essence, irrespective of how it may be framed, any work that contributes significant data and/or extends developmental thinking will be taken under editorial consideration.

Submissions should contain a minimum of 80 manuscript pages (including tables and references); the upper limit of 150–175 pages is much more flexible (please submit four copies; a copy of every submission and associated correspondence is deposited eventually in the archives of the SRCD). Neither membership in the Society for Research in Child Development nor affiliation with the academic discipline of psychology are relevant; the significance of the work in extending developmental theory and in contributing new empirical information is by far the most crucial consideration. Because the aim of the series is not only to advance knowledge on specialized topics but also to enhance cross-fertilization among disciplines or subfields, it is important that the links between the specific issues under study and larger questions relating to developmental processes emerge as clearly to the general reader as to specialists on the given topic.

Potential authors who may be unsure whether the manuscript they are planning would make an appropriate submission are invited to draft an outline of what they propose and send it to the Editor for assessment. This mechanism, as well as a more detailed description of all editorial policies, evaluation processes, and format requirements, is given in the "Guidelines for the Preparation of *Monographs* Submissions," which can be obtained by writing to Wanda C. Bronson, Institute of Human Development, 1203 Tolman Hall, University of California, Berkeley, CA 94720.